The Stranglers

1977

Laura Shenton

"Now that we've got where we have — but we're not being complacent, we're still working hard on it — it's nice to be able to say a big 'up yours' to all those who put us down, knocked us, over the last year or so."

- Jet Black, *Record Mirror*, August 1977

The Stranglers
1977

Laura Shenton

WP
WYMER
PUBLISHING
Bedford, England

First published in 2021 by Wymer Publishing
Bedford, England www.wymerpublishing.co.uk Tel: 01234 326691
Wymer Publishing is a trading name of Wymer (UK) Ltd

Copyright © 2021 Laura Shenton / Wymer Publishing.

ISBN: 978-1-912782-85-7

Edited by Jerry Bloom.

Printed and bound in Great Britain by
CMP, Dorset.

A catalogue record for this book is available from the British Library.

Typeset by Andy Bishop / 1016 Sarpsborg
Cover design by 1016 Sarpsborg.
Cover photo © Trinity Mirror / Mirrorpix / Alamy Stock Photo

Contents

Preface

The Stranglers! What a fantastic band! I trust that you will share such bias with me in reading this book. There is so much to say about them in terms of their unique contribution to music. The purpose of this book is to offer an objective insight into what they achieved in 1977 — an immensely important year for them. There were so many highs and lows worth documenting including volatile gigs and ongoing questions and controversies regarding whether or not they were a sexist band. And that's before the music comes into the picture!

In the interests of transparency and context, as author of this book I have no affiliation with The Stranglers and I have no affiliation with any of their associates. The content of this book is derived from extensive research fuelled by a passion for their amazing music as well as the hoarding of a range of vintage articles. On such a basis, if you're looking for a book that's full of intensely detailed information on anyone's personal life, you won't find it here. This book is the product of an abundance of research and it certainly feels right to collate that here in order to offer an angle on the year that many consider to be The Stranglers' best.

I want to take this opportunity to point out that in 1977, the way in which language was used — as well as the social and cultural attitudes expressed by many in the media — was a completely different animal to what it is today. In such regard, when writing this book, there were moments where I had to really think about what I should and shouldn't include. In the end, I decided to take an approach that wasn't in the vein of a revisionist historian. That is to say that, what you see is what you get; I want to offer something that favours accuracy and therefore some words and phrases make for uncomfortable reading but I stand by this because I feel it is important to represent what happened as authentically and holistically as possible.

It doesn't mean that I personally stand by any of the views of others portrayed within this book, it simply means that from a research perspective, I couldn't justify censoring things that are relevant to what was happening at the time. Read on and form your own opinion. Overall, I am keen to present what happened without painting my own bias on top of it.

This book is a gossip free zone. I want to present facts rather than all kinds of weird and wonderful speculations. Also, there will be nothing herein that is in the lexicon of "this song is in B minor so it probably means XYZ." Nope! Not happening! I want to present how the music resonated with people at the time and not what my perception of it is as one of millions of fans out there. Oh, and that reminds me, I was born in 1988 — so ages after all of this stuff happened and thus, this book is a culmination of extensive research that I intend to use objectively to offer a worthwhile narrative on, what is ultimately a vital and fascinating period in The Stranglers' career. 1977, the year that started it all...

Prologue

F ans of The Stranglers will know who the band are and their legacy is such that over the years, they have all become memorable for what they have done in their careers in the public eye. In 1977 though, they had gone from being relatively unknown to being a household name and thus for context, here is the way in which each of them were profiled by *Melody Maker* in September 1977...

Hugh Cornwell: "In 1974, Hugh Cornwell, having ditched a lucrative medical career in Sweden, came back to England to find 'three years of nothing.' That was when he felt a new band, with fresh ideas, could literally sweep to power. Cornwell, nonchalant about practically everything musical before the Year Of The Stranglers, impresses with his staunch opinion of his band's future. Prepare yourself. He intends to put fans through one endurance test after the other."

"He was raised in a Kentish Town prefab, where his parents had grand plans for their boy to become a doctor. Little Hughie, however, had other ideas. He formed his first band at Hornsey College of Art, a neatly named combo called Emil and The Detectives. Apart from Cornwell, who played bass, the band featured Richard Thompson (of Fairport and solo fame) on guitar and Nick Jones (former *Melody Maker* writer, son of Max, and now PR to the stars) on drums. For a long time, that was as far as Cornwell's musical aspirations went."

"After gaining a third-class degree in biochemistry, he split for Gothenburg in Sweden, where he worked as a laboratory assistant, and also formed a band called Johnny Sox. Nothing great but it kept his finger in the pie. Hugh, who felt that he was capable of greater things, decided to split from Sweden because he considered he was being manipulated by other doctors and was unable to get on with his own work. Perhaps one day, he ponders, he will set up his own laboratory, 'I could make some interesting substances'."

"Back in England, Cornwell had very definite ideas of the type of band he wanted to form. 'We wanted a band that would play songs more commercially orientated in the sense that we would bring back the song. The song has been sadly lacking. We wanted to revitalise it as an important music form instead of technical virtuosity. Since about 1971, the song has been slowly defused. There has been the odd thing, like Bowie producing *Ziggy Stardust*, but that was very isolated. When it came out in England, it was the only thing that was happening. One album. It was terrible. I knew that The Stranglers were going to be a success but we didn't know what form it was going to take. I knew it was going to be different. I knew it was going to be more song orientated or melody orientated'."

"'People say we're excellent musicians but we're not, you know. We just don't go beyond our limitations, so we don't show that we're limited in our skills. Everyone says that we're amazing musicians and we're not. It just shows how much you can achieve by being aware of your limits. A lot of people don't do that'."

"The lyrics, written by Cornwell with Burnel, have attracted much attention. On the *Rattus Norvegicus* album there were some fierce examples of chauvinism on 'London Lady' and 'Peaches' while the forthcoming stuff, like the next single, 'No More Heroes', has the band's lyricists taking a broader and even harsher standpoint."

"'The lyrics have been called more than chauvinistic,' a twinkle comes to Cornwell's eye, 'some people said they're dross. Some people said they're terrible. Crass lyrics, meaningless statements. They're just ahead of their time, that's all. I suppose they are threatening to some people. In 'Something Better Change', we're just saying that we want to see more action, sociological changes, structural changes, and we want it to happen quicker that it is happening. It's so slow. It always seems to end up going at the same slow pace, and then it's so slow that a lot of its activeness is defused by that pace'."

"What changes should The Stranglers bring? 'We're already bringing changes. We get banned by local councils and then they end up having to book us because the demand is too great. In our own way, we try and create as much disorder as possible. Confusion is the main thing, making people think twice about things instead of accepting stances and opinions. If you confuse them, they start re-thinking and it's good to make people re-think attitudes. The next thing we do is become unestablished, probably by using musical methods. We're going to test people's tolerance levels as to what they accept a song to be'."

"Wasn't that what The Stranglers revolted against? 'Ah yes, but maybe we can improve the concept of the song rather than destroy it. The B-side of the next single ('In The Shadows') will be musically quite anarchic because there are no verse structures. There are musical changes in it, but there are no set verse patterns and things like set lengths, and yet it is still a song and there are still things that you sing at the end because you remember them. It's sort of an experiment. We feel that we have a responsibility and an obligation as well. People are looking to the crest of the new wave for change, for breaking new ground. Innovation and all that, so we have got to push ourselves over the limits and into new ground. We have got to try and find new things, break new ground. Experiment'."

Dave Greenfield: "Dave Greenfield's listening habits of late have included doses of Camel's 'Flight Of The Snow Goose', The Moody Blues' *Days Of Future Past*, Supertramp's *Crime Of The Century* and Pink Floyd's *Dark Side Of The Moon* ('please don't tell Hugh about that one'). You read right. A member of The Stranglers actually possesses conservative tastes. But then when you talk to Dave Greenfield and acquire an understanding of his past and his attitudes, it ceases to become such a surprise."

"Greenfield doesn't have the same rebellious streak as the other three Stranglers. He is undoubtedly the most experienced musician in the band. Since leaving school in Brighton, he reckons he has drifted in and out of about thirty bands in all, occasionally taking on outside work, usually painting and decorating, to subsidise his musical aims. His climb has been quite traditional – school bands, and ventures to the attractive German market, where bands could make a living out of playing in American forces' bases and civilian clubs."

"Greenfield started off his musical career on guitar, changing to keyboards through 'events beyond my control' when, in one of his early bands, a shift within the band ended with the keyboard player on bass and Greenfield on keyboards."

"The most notable of his early bands was Rusty Butler, from Brighton, and when he left they eventually changed their name to Krakatoa, now famous as the unluckiest band in the world. It was after one of his German trips that the chance to join The Stranglers came up. The band had already been going for a year and decided to find a keyboards player and sax player, so they placed an advertisement in (where else?) the *Melody Maker* classifieds."

"Greenfield replied, turned up for the audition and got the gig. The sax player, by the way, lasted only three days. He wanted to be the front man. Greenfield agreed that he was given quite a free hand on keyboards. 'I wouldn't be happy being stuck in the background just playing chords and the odd little solo. There would be no room for self-expression, to use a very old term, it would become boring'."

"The music seemed to be more important to Greenfield than the revolutionary ideals behind it. 'I have always been into music. It is a great idea to carry an ideal, but it is the music that makes that possible. It's a combination, I imagine. The music had to change to go with the ideal'."

Jet Black: "As a child, Jethro Black (sic) was chronically ill (his diagnosis) with asthma. As a result, he missed out on much of his education ('I was always two light years behind everybody else'). He left school bitter ('they thought I was a dimbo') because he knew his own capabilities ('I won the school chess championship'), and was suddenly cured of asthma and, as you know, went on to greater things."

"Jet is now in a position of influence, and is spending much of his time giving the fingers to the establishment. The Stranglers is his vehicle. He was born in Ilford, Essex, of an English mother and an Irish father. After leaving school, he had a number of jobs including running a wholesale and retail wine company and selling ice cream. He's played in various bands before The Stranglers but 'nothing you have ever heard of'."

"Then 'I just suddenly decided that I wanted to do something positive with music. You're obviously going to ask what my influences are, and my only influence is alcohol. That drove me on.' Very nice quote. Jet decided that rock and roll was the life for him after becoming tired of the people he was meeting in the booze business. 'We came into the music business to do something different as a band. We meet a lot of phonies – managers, agents, promoters, publicans and club owners. That was the very thing that we thought, once we get going, not only are we going to change the music of the establishment, we're going to change the business as well. We've done that and we've been through a lot of shit to achieve it'."

"The Stranglers, Jet said, had it tough in the early days. Often they would be asked to leave the stage because they weren't playing "normal" music."

"They went through a period where they were never re-booked at gigs, and it was only when they were signed with Albion Management that this changed. The band, however, weren't discouraged by the initial rejection. 'Actually, it strengthened us enormously. The more we got refused or turned away from gigs or didn't get paid because they didn't like us, the more encouragement we got. It was like the situation in the last war when the more bombs the Nazis dropped on London, the more the Londoners wanted to wind up the war and defeat Germany. We believed we were right and had something to offer. Then suddenly, there was a panic to sign up new wave bands. Record company executives are not sitting behind their desks anymore. They're all out at the clubs, looking for bands because they're afraid they're going to miss the boat. So one of the big changes we've helped bring in the record side of the business is that we've got those people off their arses and doing things and that's a healthy environment in which music can evolve. Everything was so laidback a year ago'."

"How could The Stranglers continue to fulfil their ideals? 'Well, if we see that we are reaching a situation when we can't do what we feel is right, then maybe we have reached a time where we should consider doing something else for a living. The one thing we don't want to get involved in is doing a couple of gigs a year, playing to a quarter of a million people and the poor kids are sitting two miles away watching it through a TV monitor or through binoculars. We have no ambitions to exceed our technical ability or, in fact, to improve on it to any great extent. To be super technically brilliant doesn't necessarily mean you're making good music'."

"Black feels that The Stranglers have only achieved a fraction of their aims so far. That sets him off again. 'What the music business needs is good promoters and radio stations that turn out more imaginative music. We want to change attitudes. One of the things we suffered from frequently up until recently was that we were treated like shit. There are things that are wrong and must be spoken about. We're not crusaders. We're aware of what needs changing and we're not afraid of talking about it. There's too much plastic in music and in the world, too much unreality'."

Jean-Jacques Burnel: "Like fellow Stranglers' Black and Cornwell, Jean-Jacques Burnel adopts an intimidating air of petulance and abruptness when he becomes the spokesman for the band. For instance, when asked about his past, he shuts down all avenues and bluntly refuses to volunteer any information. 'It's not really relevant to The Stranglers,' he grunts, 'who wants to know about my background? Surely I am an animal of The Stranglers and anything apart from that is not relevant to anybody apart from myself.' Then the big one – 'I am what I am. I am not what I have been. These days people are always concerned with what you have been because they feel that contributes to what you are'."

"It is only when it is pointed out to Burnel that what he

is doing with The Stranglers is probably a reaction to input of the past ten years that he accedes to the request. And so we learn that Jean-Jacques Burnel, born of French parents in Notting Hill Gate, London, was kicked out of school (he insists on retaining the right not to give specifics) at the age of seventeen for bringing out a political magazine that was viewed as incitement. He was forced to take his Advanced Level examinations in a Guildford Technical college."

"This would have been in 1970, and it was around the same time that he joined a motorcycle gang in Walton-on-Thames (The Walton Hell's Angels) and discovered drugs. 'They were the only friends I could have,' Burnel said. 'All the kids at college were all hippies. I had short hair, and for some reason they wouldn't include me in their things. I was riding a bike and the other kids had cars.' So dejected, he got into riding with the bikers, and was quickly accepted into the ranks after a few nights when he went to Walton to get "initiated"."

"This involved 'just showing class', riding with the boys, getting into a few punch-ups. Nothing much. Burnel disagreed that this had quite violent overtones. It was all very friendly. But after twenty months, he and the Angels parted company. 'They were starting to do what the press expected them to do. Around that time there was a lot of press on the Hell's Angels. They were just starting to beat kids up just for the hell of it. I didn't mind a fight. We smashed up a few places. But riding after a fifteen-year-old kid to beat him up didn't appeal to me'."

"Burnel returned to college, gaining a degree in economics, but he felt cheated when it came to tackling the world again. This time there was no job for him. It was totally the reverse of being unqualified, he explained. He was overqualified. He weaved his way through a couple of jobs, one with an engineering factory working on motorbike engines, and another driving a van."

"It was through the van driving job that he met Hugh Cornwell. Cornwell asked him to join a band he was forming, sold him a bass guitar for thirty-five pounds (the one he still plays), and Burnel gave up plans to go to Japan to earn a karate black belt."

"Joining a band seemed to be 'quite an adventure.' 'There was one thing we had in common, and that was that we hated everything that was happening at the time. I saw all these poofters in their big platformed shoes. I couldn't understand it, and they were doing these long boring songs. Even now, we ignore what's happening. We are aware of what's happening, but we never wanted to adopt symbols and that's why a lot of people put us in the punk category and others don't and some people think we're the greatest band on earth and others say we're bandwagon jumping and Doors rip-offs, so it's great. All this confusion is great. With most of the bands you can say, Sex Pistols — punk band, The Clash — politically orientated punk band, but we're not in any of those categories, because we are organic people. We change all the time and we are also very intelligent. We know who we are, unlike other people. I have been wearing black leather jackets for seven years now, since I started riding motorbikes. There is a reason for wearing black leather jackets, and it's not to pose. It's to protect you'."

"Fashion is a sensitive subject for Burnel. The King's Road, a hip punk haven, is a particular target for his venomous attack on much of the trendiness of the new wave. 'We don't pose around the King's Road. The people who dig us can't afford to go into places like that. The King's Road represents the less folk aspect of what is happening in rock music. The fact that shops are making a fortune out of a fashion is so stupid. I don't like the fact that you shop at the right places and mix with the right people. It doesn't give you any depth. And if that is the attitude, then I don't want to know. For a long time, we were slated because we didn't have fancy weird clothes. We just had the clothes we always had. I don't put a lot of stock in that sort of fashion thing. I put a lot of stock in food. It's the most important thing that I would distribute my budget towards. Food is all important to me, and clothes aren't. I mean, I don't knock a bloke for the length of his hair'."

"Burnel wasn't too aware of the more luxurious trimmings that a hit album and singles had afforded The Stranglers. He was, however, becoming more paranoid, because of street encounters with nuts not in agreement with his music and philosophies. 'I think we represent the more popular aspect of a very latest movement, and the movement isn't even really a movement because it's very divided. If you talk in critical terms or in just attitudinal terms, it is very divided. It's not a corporate movement, but there is a whole scene that is quite incestuous. There's quite a lot of overlap between bands and there's quite a lot of overlap between audiences. I can see that from the audiences who come and see us. The type of people we associate with, like the Finchley Boys, are just down to earth kids. There is a false snobbery in some new wave that makes redundancy hip. Like, the Finchley Boys would like to work because they want to eat a bit better and get better holidays and have a TV. They don't think it's hip being out of work. They want to work. They don't want to get involved in inverted snobbery. I hate a lot of elitism about the new wave. There are a lot of ponces involved, and a lot of poofters, and a lot of posers who have never dirtied their hands. I don't have to say who those people are. They know. The ones who've never sored their hands. The ones who can afford flash clothes'."

Chapter One

1977, What A Year!

1977 was a year of major importance for The Stranglers. It signifies the point at which they went from being a "punk" band playing in pubs to dominating the charts throughout the year to the extent that they became a household name.

The year documents a rapid career acceleration whereby they went from being a support act at London's Roundhouse to playing to packed crowds who had come to see them exclusively. When asked his thoughts on The Stranglers' rapid rise in popularity, Burnel told the fanzine, *Shews*; "It had to happen. It was a spontaneous thing which lots of people related to. Lots of people also went off and started bands, which was great. It means that there were a lot of people who were frustrated."

1977 was the year that punk and new wave was arguably at a commercial peak. Throughout this book, the terms will be used interchangeably purely on the basis that people chose to do that when referring to The Stranglers at the time. Importantly though, the band had their own ideas about how they fitted into such genres and indeed, on how they didn't.

Regarding the term punk, Cornwell was quoted in the *Aberdeen Evening Express* in February; "It was the media who started that term, not the bands. "Psychedelic" is more valid comment on us."

He was quoted in the *Daily Mirror* in October; "We play our brand of folk music — music for the people." And in the *Sports Argus* in February; "We have disassociated ourselves from the label "punk rock". We prefer to think of ourselves as a "new wave" band. But we agree with a lot of things the punk groups say. About established rock stars for example — they just sit back in their mansions or smash up their cars. They are total parasites. A new aristocracy of musicians with power and money and influence has grown up and they have abdicated from any social responsibility. When did you last hear songs of social comment? We're writing songs about things like how it must feel to be black in Britain. And unemployment and other issues."

Black was quoted in *Record Mirror* in August; "We're new wave, but not punk. But we started a lot of the "punk" style. Like abusing the audience, throwing beer at them. Johnny Rotten and Joe Strummer were always at our early gigs, picking up tips."

It was advocated in the *Daily Mirror* in October that despite the band's aggressive bravado, "they are a peaceful lot off stage. Although they are heralded as punks, they don't particularly care for the label... In fact, it's almost as if punk has caught up with The Stranglers. For they had been playing their particular brand of music since the spring of 1975 when it suddenly became fashionable at the end of the year."

When The Stranglers released their debut album in 1977, it was one of the first (so-called!) punk albums to make a commercial impact whereby it got to number four in the UK. It was a substantial achievement considering that at the time, The Stranglers were still only a band with a small cult following.

Amongst all the bands who were considered to be under the umbrella of punk, The Stranglers were able to make a name for themselves and branch out beyond the roots of their beginnings. It could be said that The Stranglers were something of an anomaly on the basis that for some, they were too punk for the mainstream and too mainstream to be accepted by punk.

As Burnel said in *Melody Maker* in September; "All this confusion about us is great." To which Cornwell was quoted, "We are now going to test people's tolerance level."

It is easy to see how The Stranglers didn't fit in with the other punk bands, or indeed with the more established rock groups either. It was reported in the *Daily Mirror* in September; "British rock stars again dominated the *Melody Maker* readers' poll awards, which were presented in London yesterday. But punk rock — widely considered as just a passing phase — also entered the lists, with The Stranglers winning the Brightest Hope section. Apart from this, the "serious" rock bands swept most of the major honours." The article then went on to list awards that had been given to Yes, Genesis, Jimmy Page and Robert Plant. In December The Stranglers won the *Daily Mirror*'s award of the best new wave band.

When asked if he felt whether the emergence of new wave had helped The Stranglers to be accepted, Jet Black, talking to *Sideburns* fanzine in January '77 said; "We were beginning to attract attention long before the punk thing started. So I don't think it's just the new wave that has brought appreciation of our music on. It's just the fact that people perhaps are more aware, you know, the press talks about the new wave of bands so maybe more people are prepared to come and listen to what we are trying to do. I suppose in a way it does help but we were doing what we are doing now about a year ago, which was long before any talk of the new wave... I think that we were one of the first British bands to be labelled by the media as a punk band, but we've never regarded ourselves as a punk band."

"I suppose we're on the fringe of punk. I think that the whole concept of the new wave of punk bands is great because it means change, and the music over the last five years certainly has become incredibly boring with very few exceptions, especially around the small clubs and pubs. You see the same old bands doing the same old stuff and taking off each other, and the whole thing is totally stagnated. So the mere fact that a new wave of bands has emerged that are doing something different is great. I mean, it can't do any harm."

"Some of the bands are suffering from adverse publicity but this is really a storm in a teacup, it all amounts to nothing, and all these chaps are trying to do it to play something a bit different and add a bit of excitement into a very dull music scene, so that is good — and we're all for it... Punk will go on for quite a while, and you'll see bands emerging and others dropping out like with any new movement, and eventually I suppose it'll be time for something new. Who knows what that'll be."

In some ways, The Stranglers' music had a wide-ranging appeal. *Melody Maker* commented in September; "After playing something like four hundred gigs in two years, the band brought out their first album, *Rattus Norvegicus*, on United Artists and the response was phenomenal. The band's popularity soared. Not only were they lauded by the new wave, but straight rock fans dutifully bought the album."

It was considered in *Record Mirror* in June that The Stranglers' "music is immaculate, luxurious even. Arrangements severe enough to hurt/court fevered brows."

The Stranglers' self-awareness often came across in interviews. Cornwell speaking to the *Aberdeen Evening Express* in February said; "The only thing which will make the distinction in the new wave bands is commercial success. It's all right selling 2,000 copies of a record, but it's whether you can get out and let the people go with the music. If it is just going to be a cult thing it will all be completely forgotten about in a short time."

Perhaps in some ways a more mature band, The Stranglers seemed to have a sensible approach overall. Black told *Record Mirror* in August; "I get a bit bored with interviews, always being asked the same questions, but they're necessary, like playing on *Top Of The Pops*. The music press? I read all the music papers. They're all fine, and do their job, except *Melody Maker* — did you see their review of our album? It's strange, they seem to take delight in building up acts and then more delight in knocking them down. But having hits and finding success hasn't changed us. The best thing about it is the security, not having to worry about where the next meal is coming from. There were times, not so long ago, when we could barely afford the price of a bowl of soup. We don't stay in luxury hotels or ride around in Rolls Royces, we don't want to and we don't need to. We're happy to stay in hotels where we aren't kicked out at nine in the morning."

Punk had originally developed as a backlash against the musical institution of the mid-seventies that was populated by long established bands and progressive rock. Against the establishment of the music business, Burnel told the *Sunday Mirror* in June; "One day you worship someone, the next he's riding around in a Rolls Royce. Young people don't like it pushed in their faces."

Punk was designed to be more accessible; anyone could come and have a go at it and the genre was centred on an exuberance of aggression that sought to challenge the status quo. Ironically though, once it had established itself and the parameters within which it would function, punk itself became an institution, so much so that it became something of a cliché of itself; there came a point where even the Sex Pistols became part of the rockstar machine that they initially sought to challenge.

In an interview with the band's own fan club magazine *Strangled* that took place in May, Burnel was advocating for "basic respect for other individuals in the context of a society. And it seems to me that at the moment some people are trying to break down one esoteric group and replace it with another that is equally narrow minded and fascist."

Luckily for The Stranglers, although many chose to classify them as punk, they themselves were keen to assert that this wasn't the case. However, it is undeniable that being labelled as such was probably to their advantage when it came to playing up to their media image.

Regarding the punk label, Cornwell was quoted in *Louder Than War* in September 2019; "It was a double-edged sword; you have to take the rough with the smooth. In one way it was labelling and in another it was enabling, a window of opportunity. Some of the people who were included in that, like Elvis Costello, Graham Parker, Blondie, no way would you call "punk", they're just writers of great pop songs. It wasn't just us that it happened to, I mean look at The Police!"

"It was just a window of opportunity for everybody involved and you have to take any opportunity you get. It's funny because even though bands like the Sex Pistols and The Clash have stood the test of time in their musical significance, it's the artists like The Police and Elvis Costello who went on to stratospheric success and they should never have been under that label anyway."

"The notoriety helped and hindered The Stranglers. It got us on the front page of some newspapers, with some stories, which were embellished, made to sound worse than they actually were but in other ways it created obstacles. For example, we went to Australia for the first time and our tour of New Zealand was cancelled. We were really looking forward to going and were told that we were banned because the government of New Zealand didn't want people like us in their country, because of what they'd read. Notoriety worked for us and against us."

Speaking to *The National News* in January 2012 Jet Black recalled; "We were very provocative in the early days. There was all sorts of muck and vitriol written about us in the tabloids. Some of it true and some of it wasn't, but we never bothered to set the record straight. Why would we? We were selling millions of records. They called us the most hated band in rock and we were bottled on stage more than once. I think we just didn't fit in and we were probably very arrogant, but we always made good music and stayed true to ourselves."

However, it comes across that The Stranglers refused to play up to the stereotypes of punk that they didn't identify with. Burnel told *New Musical Express* in October; "I'm not from a working class background and won't pretend I am." To which Cornwell was quoted, "Everyone inventing proletariat backgrounds."

1977 was a big year for punk. Characterised by a provocative image that included spitting, body piercings, crazy hairstyles — all basically things that were designed to antagonise and to be a mark of rebellion. The musical repertoire included the release of the Sex Pistol's *Never Mind The Bollocks* as well as debut albums from the likes of The Damned and The Clash.

It was in stark contrast to the other bestselling records of that year: Fleetwood Mac's *Rumours*, Pink Floyd's *Animals*, Abba's *Greatest Hits*, The Shadows' *20 Golden Greats* and

Bread's *The Sound of Bread*. Highlights in the singles chart included Elvis Presley's 'Way Down', Donna Summer's 'I Feel Love' and Emerson Lake and Palmer's 'Fanfare For The Common Man'.

Those who did choose to categorise The Stranglers as punk seemed to do so on the basis that the group had a rebellious streak that unashamedly granted them a lot of media attention. Arguably, this perhaps played a necessary role in elevating The Stranglers to a point of fame that helped to push them commercially.

Despite this however, as was noted by a number of critics, musically, The Stranglers had something to offer that went beyond the conventions of what other punk bands were doing at the time. On instrumentation alone, they were more melodic than many of their punk peers, as is evidenced in the fact that their music made generous use of keyboards. It gave their sound a texture that offered a greater sense of character against the loud forcefulness of their songs.

Impressive considering the three minute, three chord songs from the likes of the Sex Pistols, The Damned and The Clash (that's not to say that The Stranglers were "better" than those bands because, after all, what is "better"? The point is that The Stranglers were, musically, doing something that went beyond a lot of the idiosyncrasies of punk).

When asked if he resented the Sex Pistols for the reputation that they had given the new wave, Burnel told *Shews*; "No, I don't resent them for the reputation that they've got. I just question their honesty and sincerity. The thing is, if you're going to get involved in politics, which I am personally into, then you've got to be specific about your standpoint and you've got to live the part, you can't be half hearted about it. I'm not too hot on their music, myself, I like the production of 'Anarchy' though. I also don't like the way that they pay lip-service to the American east coast bands like The Stooges and The New York Dolls — I don't rate that scene much. I don't think it's valid. The Pistols call Led Zeppelin boring old farts but they (Zep) haven't been going as long as The Stooges, who were ten years back. Your statement's gotta be true and without flaws. There's been a lot of hype about how they don't smoke dope. They do, I tell you, they do. It's crazy 'cos people will always find the truth out in the end, they will see hype for what it is. People will see through attempts at being sincere. The publicity that the Pistols have got themselves is worth a lot of records."

In 1977, The Stranglers sold more records than any other "punk" group. The year saw them release two hit albums and three singles that got into the top ten, all whilst they performed at least one hundred gigs.

As their debut, *Rattus Norvegicus* introduced the unique sound that would stay with many fans for a lifetime and it wasn't long after that the second album, *No More Heroes*, was released in order to capitalise on the popularity of the band based on what they had already achieved that year.

The power of self-belief probably goes a long way. Cornwell told *Sports Argus* in February; "Of course we're going to be big. In two years we will be so big you won't believe you ever did this interview. We have done about two hundred gigs — twice as many as other new groups like us. We get on well, we are writing profusely and everything is going well for us."

A&M American chief Martin Kirkup was quoted in *Sounds* in July; "The Stranglers have a unique sound and I'm sure American fans will take to the band in the same way that English fans have."

He wasn't wrong. It was reported in *Sounds* in

September that "*Rattus Norvegicus*, released two weeks ago by A&M in the States, has climbed to number 183 in the American charts. Don't laugh. Stateside 183 means something like 30,000 copies."

The UK success was just about starting to wedge itself open globally, not that the band had their hearts set on America at the time. Burnel, quoted in *Strangled* said; "We're certainly going to go to America but I'm not "setting my sights on America" — it's not a great ambition of any of us to woo America. (Some) see it as the be all and end all, so it depends on your motives. I mean, I started to play there about three years ago and it was an adventure for me. It was something that I thought I could contribute to. I thought I could fulfil myself."

Cornwell felt much the same as reported in *Strangled*; "I don't think I want to spend too much time over there. I think that it is a crazy place. I don't know what we can achieve over there. They might get off on the more general things that we do like 'Hanging Around' and stuff like that, but it is such a crazy place... We have to approach the venues differently."

"There seems to be two alternatives. You can play at a club like CBGB's that can get about five hundred people inside and it is a bar so no kids under eighteen or whatever, so that is one audience excluded. Then you have the huge places like with twenty thousand people in it and everybody can get in, and we don't really want to do that either. What we may do is do a gig with a radio station which they do over there and maybe play at a high school or something. But it is a problem. They don't have these medium sized gigs like the Roundhouse or the Music Machine. And you think, like New York has about ten million people in it, maybe more, and they have got one main club that anybody has heard of — Gigi's, and that's the size of the Red Cow, that's all it is, a bar." Still though, From the 5th to the 20th August, Cornwell and Black did some work promoting *Rattus Norvegicus* in America.

As with many successful bands before them, some of The Stranglers' success was plausibly down to what their media image was. Two brashly outspoken frontmen, Hugh Cornwell and Jean-Jacques Burnel, teamed with quietly brooding keyboardist, Dave Greenfield and professionally assured drummer Jet Black, The Stranglers not only sounded distinctive, but they looked distinctive too and it came across both on stage and in interviews too.

Notably, everyone in The Stranglers was quite a bit older than the members of other bands who were starting out in the punk/new wave boom. Jet Black was almost twice the age of most other musicians on the scene at the time. The journalist who interviewed Black for *Record Mirror* in August described him as "a good guy who's seen and done a lot", "gentle" and "straight talking".

It was noted in the *Aberdeen Evening Express* in February; "Being a bit older than most new wave bands The Stranglers have a tongue in cheek quality with their aggression."

In *Shews* Burnel explained how he met the others; "It's a long story. I was living in Guilford at the time, doing a van driving job. I was coming back from karate one night, in Kingston, and I met this American greaser. He happened to be lead singer for a group called Johnny Sox, which comprised of this American drummer and an English guitarist. The Americans were draft-dodgers who came over from Sweden. The English bloke was a bio-chemist. A lab assistant. The Swede was just some guy from Sweden. Hugh was the English guitarist."

"A few weeks later I met Hugh in a pub. He was getting out of his head and was moaning about the fact that everyone had left him and gone back to Sweden. So Hugh was by himself and he met this drummer called Jet Black who was a real freak, he had peroxide blonde hair and these really weird flannel drainpipes that came three inches above his ankle. At the time he was in charge of this off-licence shop. By the time he met up with Hugh and I, 'cos by then we were already thinking about two and three minute songs, Jet was letting drink and the business mix. He was getting pretty drunk."

"One day the bailiff/people from the brewery came around and chucked him out. He was more concerned with us than with the shop. Then Hugh and I dyed our hair green and red, just for the hell of it. Then we met up with Dave Greenfield. We had previously auditioned for a keyboard player, but they were all on ego trips, doing solos a la Rick Wakeman and all that shit. Dave was just right. He was psychedelic like us, experimenting with cosmic matters, man."

Black told *Record Mirror* in August; "I was into music from an early age, playing the piano and so on. I had lessons, but the family environment was not conductive to practice. I thought of going to music college, but soon decided against it. Musicians who come out of these places all play and sound the same. I was watching a school band one day and the drummer was terrible, really bad. I just went up there and said, 'Look, this is how it should be done,' and got up there and played. Soon after, I bought my first drum kit for three shillings and sixpence and slowly began adding to it."

"I started playing a few gigs and, when I left school, got a job as a shop fitter — I'd always been good with my hands. But once I'd mastered the job, I wanted to try something else. I'm that sort of person, once I achieve a goal I have to have another one to aim for. I realised there was a big demand for home brewing equipment, but no one was selling actual kits with all the necessary ingredients and bits and pieces."

"So I started doing this and business boomed up and down the country. I was even doing exporting and importing. I worked as an ice cream man. Then I decided to start my own ice cream business. That was when I moved to Guildford. I'd lived in east London until then... The business got bigger and was going really well. We were working from this four-storey building. But I was getting bored. Eventually I turned the running of the business over to my manager and told him I wouldn't be taking so much of an active role. He thought I'd gone loco when I built a sort of studio on the top floor and installed my drum kit."

"To cut a long story short, I answered an advertisement and joined this band. It wasn't exactly what I wanted, but there was something about the group. That something was Hugh. We got on well together and after a while split from the other two. One of the other two was driving back from Brighton, I think, when they picked up this hitchhiker, brought him to Guildford and asked him in for a drink. He was Jean-Jacques Burnel. We all got talking. Then a few days later, Hugh tracked down JJ and we soon established that he was keen to play bass. Hugh had a bass guitar. We tried him out and he fitted."

"To complete the line-up we decided we needed a keyboards player. We advertised and had lots of applicants, but they all thought they were another Elton John or Rod Stewart. We were just about giving up when Dave Greenfield came along... The four of us really got down to it, writing, rehearsing, scratching around for gigs. And we didn't exactly have a lot of money. Sometimes we'd have to take part time jobs. Hugh lectured at a college, Jean-Jacques taught French and Dave and myself worked as piano tuners. It was a long struggle. Some of those early gigs were disastrous... We were originally called The Guildford Stranglers. It was after we came back from a disastrous gig and someone commented, 'The Guildford Stranglers have done it again.' We argued a lot over what we should call ourselves and eventually we dropped the Guildford bit."

Regarding the band's early days, *Melody Maker* reported in September; "With a full line-up, The Stranglers hit the road, playing any gig possible, working men's clubs, anything that helped tighten up the music. It wasn't always easy and on many occasions the band were asked to leave the stage because they were playing original material that drinking customers just couldn't sing along to. The band were convinced that their own music would win through. They were often met with apathy. Their first gig at the London Roundhouse for instance, was a shambles. They were opening a Sunday bill and went onstage to find that the PA hadn't been switched on."

At one early gig, the audience walked out in droves. Jet Black told *Sideburns* in January; "It was in Purely, some sort of Conservative Club, over eighteens night, or something, and when we saw the public walking in dressed in evening gowns we thought, 'they are not going to like us' and we decided that we weren't going to compromise our act, we were just going to play what we usually played, after all, we had been booked by somebody who'd had plenty of time to see what our act was about and it wasn't really offensive — it was just that we could see that these people were just into less interesting music than we were trying to create, and to these sort of people I think that we'd only gain respectability when we were seen on the television."

"So at the beginning of the act I went up to the mic and said 'Well, you're not going to like us so you might as well fuck off now.' So after a couple of numbers a couple of people started to leave and then a few more, and towards the end of the evening they were running to the door, they didn't want to be the last ones out. All four hundred people walked out and that was tremendous because it proved to us that what we were about was what we thought we were about. That here was an audience that we could see that didn't have the perception and the interest in music to even want to listen to us and it is often very easy to assess what an audience's reaction will be to us purely by the way they behave and the way they look, so that was really good..."

"It would have been nice if they would have enjoyed us but you see, there is a large section of the population who are only interested in songs they know, and you can see them in all sorts of venues. People go along expecting to hear certain songs and in that sense it's the same for us. The fans that come to see us want to hear our songs even though they have heard them before, so obviously if you hear a sound and you like it you're going to want to hear it again, but there is a type of audience that only wants to hear what they know and love if you like, and there are other audiences that want to hear something new, you know."

"You can't play original music to the sort of audience that only wants to hear stuff that they have heard on the radio or chart material... I think people are very scared of the unknown, in fact, even when it comes down to music a lot of people are scared to sit and listen to music they don't understand. I don't know, they have a musical complex in some way."

Could it have been a self-fulfilling prophecy though? They did after all, tell the audience to fuck off at the start of the gig. Either way, I bet a lot of Stranglers fans would have loved to have been a fly on the wall at that gig.

In 1976, The Stranglers were nurturing a small following of fans, some of whom were incredibly loyal to them. One such friend was the famous Dagenham Dave. He was a working-class man originally from Manchester. His nickname was fondly given to him by The Stranglers because he had previously worked for Ford Cars in Dagenham.

Such was Dave's passion for The Stranglers music that he attended their gigs often and once offered the band full use of his girlfriend if they so required it. Something of a party animal, Dagenham Dave would go on to become an important part of The Stranglers' legacy (on a bootleg of the gig that took place at Manchester's Electric Circus on 6th June 1977, Cornwell tells the crowd that Dagenham Dave was "one of the greatest blokes you could meet.").

The Stranglers had a respectable following quite a while before their debut album came out. *Zigzag* reported in November 1976; "Among the hordes of bands currently playing London's pub and club circuit, The Stranglers are leading contenders to break out and hit unsuspecting mass audiences and the big time. In a year of solid gigging in the smoke they've built a fanatical following with their rancid brand of manic rock."

"At the time of writing the plum support spot on the Patti Smith tour and their first provincial voyages are set for the near future, so Strangler mania might well be enveloping the country by the time you read this. That would be one of the best things that could happen right now. The Stranglers untamed originality is a force nine gale of bad breath which could knock the already battered music scene into a cocked hat."

"Along with other high intensity bands like The Hot Rods, The Clash and The Rockets, and American counterparts like The Flamin' Groovies, they could prod the sleepy rock scene into throwing off its *Melody Maker* bedspread to wake up fresh and revitalised."

"The first time I saw The Stranglers they were supporting Patti Smith at the Roundhouse on the Sunday. I'd seen their name in various gig guides, but such was my pub rock conditioning that I was not expecting much more than another competent boogie outfit, and therefore missed half their set. I should have known better with a name like The Stranglers."

"The minute I entered the old engine shed I was aware that something far different and one hundred times more exciting was going down. There were these two depraved looking geezers hacking dementedly at their guitars, while a bearded character with plaited ponytail coolly produced unbelievable soaring melodies from a battered Hammond. Holding this avalanche of lunatic genius together was a thickset drummer who behaved more like he was hammering the roof on a garden shed — occasionally standing up for added force."

"They built to an awesome climax, then stopped suddenly. A short gap. The guitarist announces a number called 'Down In The Sewer' and they career into a song about making it with rats. I was absolutely stunned. It's always nice when you're pleasantly surprised by a band you had no preconceived ideas about, but there was something far stronger — and stranger — about these Stranglers. It was like some sinister force was possessing these four degenerates, ripping music beyond the capabilities of mere mortals from their convulsed forms."

The feature continued; "Such is their originality the poor old Stranglers come in for a double dose of the old comparisons when unfortunate writers like myself try to convey their unique sound on paper. Most frequently drawn-up similarities are with The Doors, Velvet Underground, Seeds and sixties psychedelic bands. I'll go along with that, so will the Strangs (sic) as these bands have definitely been past influences on the group."

"It's inevitable an organist who combines a mysterioso with melody will get compared to Manzarek, although Dave Greenfield insists he never heard much Doors before becoming a Strangler. The unrelenting viciousness of the beat to some of the numbers, as well as the unsavoury lyrics and subject matter probably evoke the Velvets comparisons. But with these basic similarities, comparisons and categorisations must end."

"The Stranglers sound like no one as much as The Stranglers (the only non-original number in the set was Burt Bacharach's 'Walk On By'). My second exposure to The Stranglers occurred at the Flamin' Groovies / Ramones bicentennial hop, again at the Roundhouse. This time they surpassed the previous gig and also got a rousing reception."

"That clinched it. I had to know more about this lot, so I scurried down to the Nashville to catch one of their Thursday night spots to talk to the band..."

"The Stranglers are based in an unlikely place called Chiddingford near Guildford, Surrey, which means they do a lot of commuting to gigs. Guildford, far from encouraging the band's endeavours, has turned against them. 'They resent us,' says Jet Black, 'Basically they just can't handle the fact that we're playing in London all the time. There's a lot of semi-pro bands down there who think they're the greatest. We don't even play there'."

According to the feature in *Zigzag* in November 1976, The Stranglers' first ever gig was at the Purley over eighteen's club annual dance. Also playing at the gig were The Rockets. Cornwell was quoted; "Three hundred and seventy-five people walked out on us at that gig. They all turned up in ultra-smart evening dress and as soon as we started they began drifting out. By the time we'd finished there were about three people left. Right in the middle of a number a guy came up and grabbed me. I thought he was going to get heavy, but he just launched into a very intellectual rap about why we weren't working with the audience, the ethnic quality of the music and bluurrgh! We just told him to piss off and kicked him off stage."

To which Burnel added, "Mind you, they just weren't our type of audience, and we did happen to be out of our heads 'cos we'd had a four hour wait to go onstage. We went on and said, 'You're not going to like us so you may as well piss off!' As the set went on it sank in and they started going out in droves, panicking at the exits."

As punk started to take off in the mainstream, by late 1976 The Stranglers gigs continued to attract large boisterous crowds. Not only was punk a musical statement, but a social one too. Even though as they came to prominence in 1977, The Stranglers were keen to make it clear that they weren't a punk band, they were often lumped in with it by the media to the extent that on one occasion, the *News Of The World* referred to Hugh Cornwell as "a brainy drop out". Notably, it took a while for The Stranglers to be respected as musicians!

It was in May 1976 that they first supported Patti Smith when she gigged at the Roundhouse in London. It was a big deal for The Stranglers, with their management, Albion having got them the job. In October 1976, they once again supported Patti Smith for one night at the Birmingham Odeon and two nights at the Hammersmith Odeon.

They were still something of an underdog group when the decision was made for them to support her again; they hadn't gone down that well with the crowd in June but it was Smith's manager, John Curd who thought highly of The Stranglers and wanted to bring them back in the October. Andrew Lauder of United Artists was present having been invited by The Stranglers management. Their performance from the Saturday night in Hammersmith was reviewed in *Sounds* the same month; "They were much improved from my last experience of them, and there is a lot in their playing, particularly Jet Black's drumming... I find The Doors reference tedious and the subject matter of their songs uninteresting. Still, as each number started I could remember the whole tune having only heard them once, it says something about staying power."

Regarding touring with Patti Smith, Burnel told *Shews*; "Out of five gigs with her, she only let us have one sound check. Subsequently, we only had one good gig. She was two hours late for the Birmingham concert, so we walked off stage after three numbers. I had one hassle with her, I went up to complain about the sound situation. I said 'Look, you better have your sound check, 'cause we're gonna have ours.' She said, 'Oh no you're not. The people don't come to see you, they come to see me'."

"That's fair enough, but I just didn't rate the attitude. I thought it was anything but a street level attitude. I don't like many of the other American new wave bands though. To me the American scene is pretty irrelevant. British journalists have got this terrible disease of paying lip-service to the Americans, they think that everything British has got to be second rate. The American writers think the other way. It's a disappointment, objectively speaking, because our bands can so often outplay the Americans and we've all got much more energy and drive..."

"We're doing a week at CBGB's in May, I think. We'll show the Americans where they should be at, 'cos they're a lot of softies. I remember when the Ramones were here, a plastic glass was chucked at the guitarist and he looked up and shouted, 'That's heavy, man,' and he rushed back to the changing room. I liked their first album though. It was really great. They've got some great rock and roll songs as well."

On touring with Patti Smith, Jet Black speaking to *Sideburns* said; "It was great for the exposure it gave us, very enjoyable gigs. We suffered a lot with equipment hassles and several times we didn't get enough time to get a sound check, so we weren't very happy with the sound at those gigs, one of them was very good — I think we did four or five with her in all, the sound just wasn't as good, but it was a great experience. It took us to an audience that we wouldn't have reached otherwise, it was good for us, good exposure."

Regarding the sound problems at the Birmingham Odeon gig, Cornwell told *Sports Argus* in February; "That was a disaster and we want to forget it."

Although The Stranglers played well live overall, Lauder was still unsure. Consequently, Albion asked Lauder to see what he thought of The Stranglers in a more neutral setting at Fulham Studios where problems with the PA system wouldn't compromise the sound and performance.

It was through this that The Stranglers signed with United Artists on 6th December 1976 for £40,000. In contrast to their reputation for being reactionary, the band used the money to invest in new equipment.

When asked who was responsible for setting up the deal with United Artists, Burnel told *Shews*; "It was really Andrew Lauder that set it up for us. He's a really great guy. He's not one of those record company types who immediately weighs up how much money a band is gonna make after seeing them. He's a fan!"

"For example, just recently he's done a Beat Merchants

compilation — it's full of bands like The Big 3, The Paramounts, The Merseybeats and The Subway Sect. I mean, basically, he's that kind of person, he even pogos. I just wish that there were a lot of A&R people like him... About a year ago Arista showed an interest. They paid for a week in the studio, but they couldn't understand or relate to us and they really didn't know what to make of us as the new wave scene wasn't as strong as it is now, in fact, there was no scene at all. It was only the Pistols and us, that was it."

Burnel also explained to *Shews* about the negative reaction to the demo tapes before UA decided to sign them; "No one was interested of course, because the music was totally alien. The record companies — all of them — didn't want to know. It was short jeans, short hair and short numbers. In fact, CBS were the first people that we sent a tape to and a guy called Dan Robbins came with Ian Hunter to a gig and they liked it so much that the next day they had a board meeting to find out why they had missed the tape before. It was such a big organisation that someone must have overlooked it."

"The same thing happened with Arista. Andrew Bailey, their A&R bloke, told us the other night that he thought that we were incredible, and now regrets not signing us up. The thing is, these people didn't have any foresight. Whereas blokes like Andrew Lauder were willing to take a gamble, like he did with the Feelgoods."

It was reported in *Zigzag* in November 1976 that after having formed in August 1975, The Stranglers "punted tapes around the agencies and record companies and were eventually signed by Dai 'Abolical' Davies of Albion." To which Jet Black was quoted, "Dai was intelligent enough to see that we were immensely talented." Dai got the band a number of gigs which resulted in some record companies taking an interest. At the time the article was written, a demo tape of 'Go Buddy Go' was being circulated to record companies.

On 28th January 1977, The Stranglers released their debut single, '(Get A) Grip (On Yourself)'. It didn't quite scale the heights that the band would enjoy later that year. It got to number forty-four in the UK. It is worth noting though that there were some dodgy calculations involved when it came to how the chart was worked out with regards to this single; it was actually the case that some of the sales of 'Grip' were attributed to a different and unrelated single that was in the charts at the time.

Ultimately, an admin cock-up that was only taken into account after the fact. Still though, The Stranglers were on their way, so much so that upon the release of the single, the band noticed a marked increase in crowd enthusiasm when they played the song at the Penthouse Club in Scarborough in late February.

The single had been given radio airplay, which must have helped to get the word out. On the advert for the '(Get A) Grip (On Yourself)' single, The Stranglers were introduced by United Artists as follows: "Tipped for success in 1977 by papers as diverse as *The Sun*, *The Guardian*, *Sounds* and NME, The Stranglers look set to become the most interesting of all the "new wave" London bands. The first recording of the band features two of their best known stage numbers. Described by one critic as 'a force nine gale of bad breath', The Stranglers will be huge, possibly very soon. The single is packaged in a special picture sleeve."

The *Liverpool Echo* said in February; "Of all the new wave bands doing the rounds at the moment, The Stranglers seem to have the most creative staying power. Their double A-side debut single featuring 'Grip' and 'London Lady' is one of the most exciting singles to come from a new wave band for a long time. For sheer energy, it takes some beating and looks like being a top twenty entry."

It was always going to be a bumpy ride. Not long after the release of their debut single, during a gig at the Rainbow where The Stranglers were playing as the special guest band for the Climax Blues Band, Greater London Council stepped in and cut the power during their set. All because they didn't like the fact that Hugh Cornwell was wearing a t-shirt with the word "fuck" printed on it in the style of the Ford logo.

It was reported in *Record Mirror* on 5th February that The Stranglers "were faded out at their London Rainbow concert on Sunday night when they supported the Climax Blues Band. It appears that the theatre's management had stipulated that no bad language should be used on stage nor should guitarist Hugh Cornwell wear his t-shirt displaying a certain four letter word. Cornwell wore the offending t-shirt. The lights were dimmed and the power cut off during the band's final number, as the band played to the 2,300 audience which included two Greater London Council councillors, one of which was the chairman of the entertainment board, Mr John Branningan. A spokesperson for the band said, 'The band are bemused that something so trivial could stop a show'."

Wow! All that. Over a fucking t-shirt! It's crazy to think that someone choosing to stop the show partway through could have been more likely to insight riots, danger and swearing than the offending t-shirt itself!

The following analysis of the t-shirt situation is arguably the most intelligent one, particularly in how it distances The Stranglers from the reputation of other bands. The *Newcastle Journal* reported in June 1977; "Wednesday was going to be a night of double pleasure for new wave fans in Newcastle with The Stranglers at the City Hall and the infamous Sex Pistols at the University. But the Pistols have unfortunately pulled out of their gig, leaving the Stranglers without any competition on the night."

"One of the more respected and musically varied new wave bands, The Stranglers have nevertheless had their almost obligatory quota of controversy with their concert at London's Rainbow being cancelled because guitarist Hugh Cornwell displayed a four-letter word on his t-shirt. But such things only tend to take attention away from the music — which after all is what it's all supposedly about. And The Stranglers, with an enjoyable first album receiving deserved acclaim, have a lot to offer in that field."

Although The Stranglers were banned by the Greater London Council for a while thereafter, it was excellent publicity. They certainly managed to upstage the Climax Blues Band and there was a lot of media coverage on the event, thus elevating The Stranglers' profile and indeed, reputation.

The start of February was tainted with a sad event in the form of Dagenham Dave's suicide. Dave had been a loyal follower of The Stranglers from their early days when they had played at the Golden Lion pub in Fulham back in early 1976. He had become a close friend of theirs. An eccentric character and an intelligent person who had his issues, the death of Dagenham Dave had an effect on The Stranglers, so much so that he would go on be paid tribute in song form.

On a brighter note The Stranglers' gained publicity via BBC Radio One's late night John Peel show. DJ Peel had been with the station since its launch in 1967. Peel's original show *Top Gear* had always been renowned for covering new bands and for his personal enthusiasm for such. Whilst a year or so earlier listeners would have more than likely tuned in to hear acts such as Be Bop Deluxe, Thin Lizzy or Caravan, by late '76 Peel had already started to embrace the new acts and cast aside the old.

The Stranglers' first John Peel session was recorded on 1st March and broadcast on the 7th (and again on 16th April). It was a match made in heaven considering that Peel was keenly promoting new wave music at the time. Four tracks were played in the session ('Hanging Around' 'I Feel Like A Wog', 'Goodbye Toulouse' and 'Something Better Change') and it gave The Stranglers a commercial boost because doing a session with Peel came with credibility. This was vital for The Stranglers at this still tentative time in their tenure. Shortly before the release of their debut album, The Stranglers played at London's Paris Theatre in the same month. It was recorded by the BBC as part of their *Live In Concert* series.

Prior to the release of *Rattus Norvegicus*, a launch party was held. Cleverly, the event took place at the Water Rat in London's Kings Road. The venue was situated a very short distance from the Sex Pistols headquarters, The Sex Shop. Burnel made the decision not to attend on the basis that, as he revealed in later years, he "couldn't be arsed."

This is something that the press picked up on. *Rattus Norvegicus* was released on 15th April 1977. A nine-track album including the single, 'Grip', it rapidly shot up the charts and into the top ten where it peaked at number four. Not bad going considering that it entered the chart at number forty-six! It was unexpected given that The Stranglers were still predominantly a London pub scene based band and had had their expectations set by some of the hostility they had experienced even in that scene.

Black was quoted in the *Daily Mirror* in October; "We had a big following before the first record. Mind you, we were booed off stage more than most bands. But we left in defiance, not in defeat. We were determined to play what we wanted and not what was expected. We knew we were on our way when we started to get second bookings."

'Peaches' was released as a single in early May. It was released as a double A side with 'Go Buddy Go' – Burnel had written the song when he was around fifteen or sixteen (it was inspired by the Beach Boys and Hendrix's 'Hey Joe'.

The reggae style present on 'Peaches' is no coincidence; it was written after they felt inspired having loaned their PA to a reggae gig in west London. They had picked up on the predominance of the bass and the syncopated rhythms. When they got back to Chiddingford, they were bursting to recreate that sound.

They made it their own though; unlike most reggae, their use of the snare isn't on the third beat of the bar. 'Peaches' continued to go up in the charts until it peaked at number eight. For commercial success to be possible, they had to censor some of the lyrics in order to get radio airplay. It was originally planned that the single would be released in a picture sleeve with a photo of the band where the song title was written in the cut up newspaper, blackmail style font.

The idea was that of United Artists. However the band objected to the lettering and it's similarity to the Sex Pistols. Although the sleeves were destroyed a few copies leaked on to the market. Consequently it is now a very rare collector's item today.

'Peaches' was reviewed in *Sounds* in May; "Rap over loutish thug riff. There should be more expression in the vocals, more *attitude*. Another reminder that this isn't a perfect world. But the track snarls compellingly enough to make an impact. Sounds like Frank Zappa without Zappa. Not a patch on the last one."

It was reviewed in *Record Mirror* in the same month; "The poet that wrote this is obviously completely uninfluenced by Dylan Thomas or T.S. Eliot. The music however, is reminiscent of several other pieces. No matter, it'll be a hit."

Mid May and it was time for the Rats On The Road tour to commence. The success of the debut album was such that they were now attracting larger crowds but unfortunately, as part of that, there was resistance from local councils who weren't happy to welcome the band to venues in their constituency.

Despite this, a tour that spanned at least thirty dates was practically sold out in no time at all. Disappointingly though, some of the dates were cancelled by the overzealous councils who were all too keen to lump The Stranglers in with how they viewed the behaviour of other bands who had played in the same venues beforehand. On balance though, the fact is that there were Stranglers gigs that were not without problems (more on that later on).

When it came to going on *Top Of The Pops* in May, although a radio-friendly version of 'Peaches' was available, it was still considered too edgy to be broadcast on TV. As a result, it was 'Go Buddy Go' that was performed on the show.

By the late seventies, when it came to getting an invite to go on *Top Of The Pops*, some bands turned it down on the basis that they saw it as "selling out" or "becoming part of the establishment". Although that generation of musicians had grown up with the programme and were aware of the high regard in which it was held, some considered that it would compromise their image rather than elevate it.

It is plausible that this is something that The Stranglers were mindful of, but when it came down to it, in terms of getting the commercial exposure to empower them to take things further, they agreed to go on the show. It would have been a big deal what with there being only three TV channels in Britain at the time.

When they arrived at the studio they were keen to rebel against the expectations that the BBC had of them. The latter had been advised to keep a careful eye out for The Stranglers so in order to blow some minds, the band asked for some cleaning materials and a vacuum cleaner; it was their tongue in cheek way of showing the producers that despite their reputation, they were not there to trash the dressing room!

It was reported in *Sounds* in June that after being taped for *Top Of The Pops*, The Stranglers travelled by helicopter to get them to a benefit gig at Colchester University in aid of prisoner's rights where five hundred pounds was raised.

The first half of '77 saw The Stranglers firmly establish themselves as strong contenders and as the second half of the year got underway, there was no stopping them. In early July the band went to TW Studios in Fulham to record songs for what would become their second album, *No More Heroes*. They recorded on a twenty-four track machine that was relatively new to the small studio.

During the sessions, the Finchley Boys were in regular attendance, smoking dope and drinking heavily. There were so many of them that, considering the small size of the studio, Martin Rushent eventually had to ask them to leave because it made it difficult for him to work there. Conveniently, a lot of the songs that appeared on that album had already been recorded during the sessions for *Rattus Norvegicus*. Just as well considering how hard The Stranglers had been working.

Black told *Record Mirror* as published in August; "The last six months in particular have been hard going, but worth it. It's been nice to have a few days' holiday. In between touring, we want to get into the studio to cut the next single, we've already decided on one side of it."

On 23rd July, The Stranglers' third single was released. It was another double A side containing 'Something Better Change' and 'Straighten Out'. The reasoning behind this was that the band weren't keen on the idea of having a song feeling like something of a throwaway B-side.

'Something Better Change' was given more radio play. Even though music videos weren't common at the time, they were made for both of the songs on the single. The footage was filmed at Notting Hill. The single was a success reaching number nine in the UK.

Due to The Stranglers' previous output, the single had been highly anticipated even prior to its release. It was reported in *Melody Maker* in July that as well as having been awarded a silver disc for the sales of their debut album, the 'Peaches' single had sold more than 170,000 copies on its way up the singles chart. Also, 'Something Better Change' had at least 11,000 advance orders prior to being released.

It was announced in the *Liverpool Echo* on 22nd July; "The Stranglers, who seem to be the thinking man's new wave outfit, release a new single today. It's a double A-side featuring the two tracks which were the "fave rave" of the recent road tour – 'Something Better Change' and 'Straighten Out'."

The *Daily Mirror* reviewed the single on the Monday 25th of that month; "The Stranglers are lovable as ever, yelling 'Stick my fingers straight up your nose.' Fans will love it."

In August, 'Something Better Change' was at number fifteen and 'Peaches' was at number twenty-eight. When asked how he felt about having two singles in the top thirty, Jet Black was quoted in *Record Mirror*; "It's good.

We've worked for it."

With all the songs for their second album in the bag, they endeavoured to play a low-key gig just for their friends, close associates and the Finchley Boys. It took place at the Herbert Wilmot Youth Centre in, of course, Finchley on Saturday 27th August. To keep the event as low key as possible the Finchley Boys worked hard to keep journalists and photographers away from the venue.

All the same, the event was packed full of revellers, some of whom were at least four hundred Finchleys! Appropriately though, the gig was held as a nod to them for sticking by the band since the early days.

On 30th August, it was back to the BBC studios where their second session for John Peel was recorded. They played 'Dead Ringer', 'No More Heroes', 'Burning Up Time' and 'Bring On The Nubiles'. For the latter, they changed the lyrics as the original ones would have been too offensive for the BBC. By this stage, The Stranglers were familiar with the songs and played them with an evident extent of exuberance.

By September, they embarked on a small tour of Europe. It included some dates in Sweden. They were met with some unwanted attention in the form of a gang known as the Raggare. The latter had a strong dislike towards British punk rock and were adamant on making their stance clear. They had something of a rockabilly image, with greased back hair and old American cars. Culturally, they represented the exact opposite of punk.

As the only band flying the flag for the music on that occasion, The Stranglers were on the receiving end of a level of violence that saw at least fifty cars turn up to break through the fencing of the venue, a large wooden chalet. The Raggare beat up The Stranglers' crew and damaged the band's equipment. In retaliation, they petrol bombed one of the offending cars. Such was the damage that when the police turned up to escort The Stranglers and their crew from Helsingborg to Copenhagen, it became clear that the gig for the following night in Stockholm would have to be cancelled. Undeterred, Burnel told the *Daily Mirror*; "In Sweden we had to cut our tour short because of an attack by the Raggare – a gang of motorised teddy boys. They injured three of our road crew and caused £4,000 of damage to our sound equipment. But we'll be back there and next time we'll be ready for them."

Besides, there was still everything to play for. It was reported in *New Musical Express* on 1st October; "The fracas was front-page news in all the Swedish daily papers, coming soon after a similar – though not so severe – attack on the Sex Pistols during their recent tour of the country. Not surprisingly, The Stranglers cancelled the rest of their dates in Sweden and flew home Thursday. Although still shaken, they are going ahead with their British tour as planned. The band's first album, *Rattus Norvegicus*, officially went gold this week. It is still strongly placed in the top thirty after twenty-two weeks and, based upon the NME Annual Chart Points Table, it is currently the eighth best-selling album of the year – with every likelihood of this placing being improved."

On 16th September, the 'No More Heroes' single was released. In response to this, *New Musical Express* advocated that "The Stranglers now set the standard against which the rest of the new bands have to measure themselves."

It got to number eight in the UK. Burnel came up with the riff and the melodies and Cornwell had already written the lyrics having recently read *Don Quixote* (which features the character, Sancho Panza). On the other side of the single was a track called 'In The Shadows'. A jazzy experimental number that had been developed in the studio during a jam, it was very different from the feel of the album that it ultimately wouldn't be included on. The track was originally twelve minutes long and the vocals and rhythms were inspired by the music of Captain Beefheart. In later years Burnel recalled that it took seven hours for producer Martin Rushent to edit 'In The Shadows' down into something that could be put onto the back of the 'No More Heroes' single. Burnel's then girlfriend rolled them a lot of joints to get them through the night with it. Cornwell explained to *Record Mirror* in September; "On the B-side of the single — well, it's a double A-side, but it's the one that won't get played very much, I'm sure, is 'In The Shadows', a very rhythmic, experimental piece of music with lot of synthesiser."

Burnel was quoted in the same feature; "It's going to freak everyone out because it's totally unexpected. It's got to change, because it's getting like a parody of itself in Britain, and things mustn't get stale."

Mid-September saw the band head out on what would be their next major UK tour of the year. The tour consisted of close to forty dates, with the final ones being at the Roundhouse. This tour had less problems with bans and cancellations, presumably because by this point in the year, The Stranglers had more credibility based on what they had achieved thus far.

Keen to support up-and-coming fellow artists, it was on this tour that The Stranglers welcomed a number of bands as support acts on various dates up and down the country. The list of bands included Radio Stars, Penetration, The Drones, Rezillos, Only Ones, Steel Pulse, The Saints, and The Dictators, who all played approximately four or five dates each. American band The Dictators were shocked to find out that it wasn't uncommon for UK audiences to spit at the bands onstage.

Late September they were welcomed back onto *Top Of The Pops* where they performed 'No More Heroes'. This time around, rather than make a mockery of the miming requirements that so frustrated them when they first appeared on the show, they took their performance seriously (well, mostly — Burnel wafted the smoke away with a newspaper instead of playing bass. In the same vein, Cornwell performed his guitar solo with one hand on the guitar and the other waving around in the air).

By this point in their careers, the tables had turned and they were more commercially established. Perhaps they were less keen to bite the hand that feeds. That said, in later years, Burnel admitted to (unsuccessfully) trying to get laid with one of Pan's People.

It wasn't long after their appearance on *Top Of The Pops* that month that *No More Heroes* was released. Coming out just five months after *Rattus Norvegicus*, the whole album is bursting with energy. It peaked at number two in the UK. The wreath design on the album cover was described as "chocolate boxy" by one journalist. It turns out that the design had been rushed on the basis that the original idea had been rejected because it only included Burnel as he posed for a photo on (a replica of) Trotsky's tomb.

The Stranglers success was such that by November, things had come full circle when they played to packed crowds at the Roundhouse. They had come a long way since the days of Patti Smith telling them that they were nothing more than her support group. By this stage in the game, The Stranglers were pulling in crowds that rivalled what The Who and The Rolling Stones had attracted to the Roundhouse.

Late November and for The Stranglers, it was back to the Hope and Anchor. The London venue had hosted them many a time in their earlier days. The gig was the opening night for what was to be the month-long Front Row Festival. It welcomed a number of bands in order to raise funds to save the venue. It was under threat of closure at the time.

The venue's landlord was Fred Grainger. The Stranglers were happy to support his cause as a way of saying thank you to him for the support he had given them when they were starting out and looking for gigs. The Stranglers' full set was recorded and later released by EMI in 1992. It's an absolute gem, featuring some of their less commonly played songs such as 'Choosey Susie', 'Tits', 'Mean To Me' and 'Walk On By'.

In response to the accusations that their two albums released in 1977 were sexist, in December Burnel posed for an implied nude photoshoot that was displayed as a centrefold in *New Musical Express*. The point of the exercise might have fallen a bit flat on the basis that, as with The Stranglers' music, it was taken in several different ways.

In later years Burnel revealed that the feature increased the attention he was getting from both women and men. The intention was perhaps in the right place though (whatever that is!) — Burnel had posed with a book that made a nod to feminist literature but when *New Musical Express* published the photos, they missed that vital bit out! Sounds like it could have been a bit of a set up there. Either that, or a misunderstanding.

It comes across that there were many occasions in which The Stranglers may have had to prove themselves. The *Daily Mirror* reported in October; "Their first album, *Rattus Norvegicus*, went to number four in the charts within days of release and has now gone gold having sold £500,000 worth of copies. Within three days of the release of the latest LP, *No More Heroes*, last month sold £250,000 worth of copies and had gone silver. Despite their success they are still banned from some hotels because they are known as punks... The most notorious thing The Stranglers did in Coventry was to play a game of pool with the locals."

Burnel was quoted in the same feature; "Because of the publicity about punks and because of the behaviour of one particular punk group – and it's not the Sex Pistols – in hotels, we still have trouble getting bookings. We are banned from so many places it is hard to credit."

During the final trip to a recording studio in late '77, they put down two songs that would go on to be released on a single in January 1978 – '5 Minutes' and 'Rok It To The Moon'. Videos were filmed to accompany both songs. They were so rowdy when they got to the film studio that Ian Dury, who was working on something in the same studio at the time, popped round to ask them to keep the noise down. A brave move considering The Stranglers' reputation at the time, but something that the band respected.

Just before Christmas, The next visit to a studio would be in the form of Bearshanks in Oundle near Peterborough, where work was started on their third album. Burnel spent some time in the studio on his own over that period because he was the only one without his own place by that point. Whilst writing the music for 'Toiler On The Sea', he had one of the Finchley Boys play the drums, albeit not very well!

1977 was characterised by two successful albums and four singles. That's before considering their sold out tours, time spent in the studio and prolific songwriting. It was the year that they arrived. People's perceptions of them had changed since their early days of being the underdog. *Rattus Norvegicus* stayed in the charts for the whole of the year since its release in the April. They had made a massive impact on the UK as well as having played in Sweden and Holland too. And that's all before America had been considered a serious contender in the equation.

The Stranglers 1977

Chapter Two

Rattus Norvegicus

Rattus Norvegicus made a strong impact in the UK. Not only did it showcase The Stranglers' musical originality but it was also the subject of some controversies based on how the media responded to it. Loathed by some, and loved by others, as a debut album it sold extremely well.

By the mid-seventies, a number of new bands were considering the merits of the live album. In particular, Dr Feelgood got to number on in the UK with theirs, *Stupidity*. It consisted of material that was recorded during a tour in 1975.

In the same vein, United Artists endeavoured to record The Stranglers performing live on the basis that their sound in such context was abundant in a raw aggression that really got through to the punters.

Burnel was quoted in *The Quietus* in March 2014; "We felt a change in the air when Hugh and I went to see Dr Feelgood in Guildford and my jaw dropped! It wasn't very sophisticated music but fuck me, it really threw a punch! We realised that this is what rock and roll should be. Not like all these long-haired guys with loads of pedals and who were up their own arses. But there was definitely a change because things were quirkier, not just stuff like country rock."

There was an element of chance involved in how The

Stranglers developed their unique sound. Burnel had a bass cabinet about the size of a door with around sixteen or so ten-inch speakers inside it. They were all a bit too small to cope with the bass and eventually they all broke. Importantly though, they didn't break beyond the point of use; it turned out that blown speakers made a dirty, deep kind of sound when Burnel continued to play bass through them.

Added to this, the complexity of some of his riffs (for example, the section that repeats to a fade on 'Straighten Out') played with power and aggression are a key feature of many Stranglers songs. Whilst many bass players are in the background, there are many Stranglers songs in which Burnel's was at the forefront.

Regarding what would be on their debut LP, Jet Black told *Sideburns* in January; "There will be songs that you are familiar with, and some new ones. We've loads of new ones in the pipeline, the problem at the moment is getting time to rehearse them, but we have all the ideas there... We have got over two hundred songs at the moment, some are just sitting there, some we've played, some we haven't, and some we are leaving for a later stage when with new equipment we can get ideas together that will suit those songs. And some songs are those that really aren't suitable for us that maybe we'd like to give to other bands, you know."

"I think we've got so many songs, we must have a song for every band in this business... We've probably done more gigs this year than anybody, and although that's nice — it keeps us in front of the public and it reaches more people — we want time to turn out records as well because people are forever asking us and right from the early days there were always people saying 'when are you getting your record out? We really like your songs, we want to hear them at home.' So obviously if you're in the music business you want to sell records."

When it came to working with The Stranglers in the studio, United Artists were very aware that it would take some thought in terms of being able to replicate the band's live sound on record. It was for this reason that initially, the idea was for their debut album to be a live one. It was going to be called *Dead On Arrival* but it never happened.

Not only was the title considered to be dull and negative but it was also the case that whenever the band tried to record a live gig, it was considered that it wasn't of a quality deemed right for a debut album. With all of this in mind, it made sense to record the debut album in a studio; it would give everyone the opportunity to get all of the tracks sounding as good as they possibly could do.

Producer, Martin Rushent, speaking to *Sounds* in September said; "We use the equipment in unorthodox ways that would be frowned upon by whoever designed them originally. As far as I'm concerned, the idea is to recreate the vibe I get off the band at a live gig and to compensate for the fact that you can't actually see the band playing in your front room. What tricks are used to make the right noise. If somebody notices any of them merely as effects then I think I've failed... When you get down to it, the sound and emotion of a record is only as good as the ingredients your artiste puts into it. All the producer does is mix the cake. So if you're working with a band that doesn't know what they want you're in real trouble."

Fortunately for everyone, the straight-up honesty of The Stranglers made them easy to work with in the studio. Jet Black said; "When we come into the studio we have a preconceived idea of what we want. It's a certain sound we get live when we've got a good sound and the acoustics are right. That's what we're looking for."

When asked what happened to the prospect of a live album, Burnel told *Shews*; "The idea of a live album is still alive, they're going to use some of the tracks spasmodically, and United Artists are also going to do a compilation LP, which would be using live recordings of gigs, taken at like six-month intervals which is going to be quite interesting."

By the time The Stranglers got into the studio to record, all of the material was put down very quickly over six days. Having played so many gigs everyone was familiar with the material. It's not that The Stranglers were familiar with the studio (they weren't!) it's that they knew their songs inside out by the time it came to getting them on record. TW Studios' engineer, Alan Winstanley contributed to the recording process as well as Martin Rushent.

Rattus Norvegicus is a memorable album – abundant in catchy songs that are played with a pulsing aggression. From the opening number, 'Sometimes', to the eight-minute closing track, 'Down In The Sewer', the album is heavy, thumping and driven. In later years, Burnel revealed that 'Sometimes' was inspired by The Doors' 'Love Her Madly'. Lyrically, there was much for the media and some feminists to complain about.

'Sometimes' is about a guy smacking his girlfriend's face. In such regard, it is understandable as to how The Stranglers came to be branded as sexist and violent because truthfully, the opening track represents a generous serving of both. However, Cornwell explained in later years that the song isn't about glorifying the violence, it is about the sadness and regret felt by the man having lashed out at his girlfriend upon finding out that she had been cheating.

According to Cornwell's stance on the song, it seems to be about the sadness of the situation rather than any kind of celebration of it. On balance though, 'Sometimes' is a bold song; a) it is completely understandable as to why some may find it offensive and b) it raises questions straight away as to whether it is the place of a band to moralise on any subject (or indeed, whether it is right for anyone else to look to a band to do so). Still though, considering that for many people, 'Sometimes' would have been their first impression of The Stranglers, the impact of the opening track on *Rattus Norvegicus* is not to be underestimated.

Whilst it matters not to negate how harmful sexism and domestic violence is, in terms of how some chose to label The Stranglers as misogynistic, it is important to take into account what the social and cultural landscape looked like at the time; it wasn't necessarily an issue that was exclusive to The Stranglers. The objectification of women wasn't uncommon in many circles and the feminists who were keen to put a stop to it were, by some, considered to be part of an angry and reactionary minority.

Of course, this is a sweeping generalisation that I am keen to state with tremendous caution here, but the point it this: the seventies were a different time with different values, where to many, women were referred to as "birds" and page three was there to be enjoyed as a bit of harmless fun. In terms of 'Sometimes', The Stranglers were bold to do it and it is plausibly part of their overall stance as a band who were keen to make a social commentary on life as they saw it; rightly or wrongly, the fact is that some men did see women as sex objects and it is something that The Stranglers picked up on in a number of their songs.

The blatant sexism in The Stranglers' lyrics was considered in *New Musical Express* in October as being "as progressive as burning witches and the widespread success is indisputable proof (as if you *still* needed it) that large numbers of this nation's youth are as reactionary, repressed and retrogressive as their parents" but that "pre-wrapped misogyny is much loved by girls too — the ones that desire a libido that's pushing the exploration of sexual cruelty to the very limit of human pain/pleasure endurance. But here it's strictly third-hand thrills, voyeuristic and vicarious."

Upon its release, *Rattus Norvegicus* invited complaint from some and considering what The Stranglers' public image was overall from their gigs and some of their interviews, it is understandable as to how (even though it might all have been a bit tongue in cheek) they were never destined to be everybody's cup of tea. Still though, as Burnel was quoted in *Strangled* from an interview that took place in May; "Sometimes a piece of music can be more powerful than words. The medium is still music."

'Goodbye Toulouse' is an exploration of the predictions of a French psychic who claimed that one day Toulouse would be the victim of a nuclear explosion. It's an intense rocker. Burnel's lyrics — where he also wove in a medieval story about a girl in Toulouse who was paraded on her balcony — were combined with Cornwell's chords to create a memorable song in 6/8 time.

Jet Black told *Sideburns*; "Nostradamus is very interesting — his predictions are uncannily correct. His prediction is that Toulouse would get wiped off the face of the earth by some sort of nuclear holocaust so it seemed a good cue for a lyric, so we wrote about that." Also though, Burnel said the lyrics of 'Goodbye Toulouse' are "about a town in France that banned us."

The overall characteristics of 'London Lady' arguably come the closest to a punk song on *Rattus Norvegicus*. Burnel's bass line is frantic against Cornwell's demanding melody. When asked if all of the songs on the album were written in response to a real event, Burnel told *Shews*; "Oh yes, they are all real. They're not just out of blue skies and about falling in love and crap like that. 'London Lady' is about three young ladies who happen to be time-wasters. They're just chicks who hang around the whole time. They rot away, they're the city's chicks. They're negative. They just sleep all day and get out of their heads."

In the same interview, when asked "What is that lyric on 'London Lady' about a plastic straw that everybody's asking about?" Burnel responded; "A lot of people ask that question and I usually tell them where to put it as well. It's about the time a year ago when lots of so-called new wavers were wearing plastic and that to me is pretty sick because plastic symbolises the whole industrial mess because industry is totally fuel orientated, that's the crux of a lot of our problems – oil. The word plastic has come to mean many different things like: 'unreal'. Like if I started wearing plastic, I'd feel like I was real sick."

'Princess Of The Streets' is reminiscent of a Doors track, so much so that as lead vocalist on the song, Burnel admitted that his contribution was something of a Jim Morrison impression. The song is in 6/8 time. In later years, Cornwell explained that Burnel had written it about a relationship he was in prior to joining The Stranglers.

'Hanging Around' has something of an acid rock feel to it. Interestingly, it wasn't uncommon for The Stranglers' sound to be described as psychedelic and this is something that they also agreed with. The interplay between the whole band – the way the song is layered and how the texture is polyphonic – certainly puts a psychedelic sound across. The psychedelic influences are probably not a coincidence. At the time, Cornwell was listening to guitarist Steve Hillage, whose 1975 solo album, *Fish Rising*, was high in psychedelic content.

When it was released as a single, 'Peaches' was an instant hit for The Stranglers. After peaking at number eight it remained in the UK top forty for fourteen weeks

— not bad for a song that the band had written two years previously! The radio edit of 'Peaches' was a necessity on the basis that the song originally made use of the words "shit" and "clitoris". Ignore that for a moment though — what a groove! Cornwell and Burnel were inspired to write the lyrics after spending some time in a club in Peckham. In later years, Cornwell asserted that 'Peaches' wasn't an endorsement of eyeing up women on the beach, it was making fun of it.

'Ugly' is unrelenting; full of pounding rage with references to acne and sulphuric acid. In later years Cornwell noted that the views expressed in the song are very subjective and that he would hope that with hindsight Burnel, who penned and sang the lyrics, would feel differently about life now. In terms of structure, 'Ugly' is probably the loosest on the album. The lyrical themes in 'Ugly' are centred on the idea of how (according to Burnel) attractive women always went for the ugly men, as long as they were rich.

As the closing track, 'Down In The Sewer' is in four parts ('Falling ', 'Down In The Sewer', 'Trying To Get Out Again' and 'Rats' Rally'). The variety of musical ideas on this track is demonstrative of how The Stranglers had more to offer than the punk bands that they were often linked with at the time.

'Down In The Sewer' was written over a significant period of time. Burnel initially had the riff — he had written it to sound like something by Captain Beefheart. The other ideas were added over a year with Burnel taking most of the responsibility for melody and Cornwell writing the lyrics. Burnel was quoted in *Louder Than War* in March 2011; "(Captain) Beefheart was hugely influential on The Stranglers and no one has ever realised that... The 'Down In The Sewer' riff is from Beefheart and loads of other stuff

— like on 'In The Shadows' where we both tried to emulate Beefheart's Howlin' Wolf voice. You can tell Hugh's voice more than mine because mine is out of its register!"

Martin Rushent's approach to recording was clever, but relaxed. The same setup was used for each song and it was simply a case of making sure that no mics had been moved when it came to starting recording again the next day. Each day would begin with a run-through and then three performances were played back-to-back before moving on to the next bit. Everything was pretty much pre-set and it made it easy to get everything recorded quickly, even though some takes were edited together in order to get the best one and there were overdubs done.

Overall, with the exception of some sound effects (the rat sound effects on 'Down In The Sewer', Rushent's idea, and the explosion sound effects on 'Goodbye Toulouse'), the recording process captured the band's collective sound, as was apparent when they played live. It was Rushent who suggested that guitar overdubs were done on 'Grip', something that gives the song a stark vibrancy.

For the fun of confusing people, *Rattus Norvegicus* was called *Rattus Norvegicus IV.* The album's back cover art is striking due to the image of the rat running along the background of a deep orange sunset underneath The Stranglers' distinctive logo. The front cover photo of the band was taken in a mansion in Blackheath. Dimly lit, the same location had been used for a number of hammer horror films.

Although the rat motif and the logo are powerful images, United Artists wanted the band to be on the cover of the record as a means of introducing them to their audience. It seems that the decision to call the debut album *Rattus Norvegicus* was something of a last minute one. It wasn't until March 1977 that *Record Mirror* announced that the album would no longer be going by the title of *Dead On Arrival*.

When asked how the album title was conceived, Burnel told *Shews*; "It's the Latin for a common rat. It can mean quite a few things. I suppose it really means that a person living in an urban society these days is like being a rat — you have the same problems. A lot of problems quite like those that rats go through."

According to *Sounds* in April, the launch party for *Rattus Norvegicus* went something like this: "Last week at Chelsea's Water Rat hostelry, The Jam were there sipping Rat Cocktails, Chelsea were there slavering over Rat Curry, and lots of people fell over. Wilko Johnson said he'd come but didn't, but everyone who did come had a jolly good time. Also conspicuous by his absence was Jean-Jacques Burnel of The Stranglers. And why not? 'Apparently he don't like liggers. Also conspicuous by his absence, the new look, Ted-style J. Rotten, who's been making a habit of turning up at the ligs after shows he hasn't seen. Wemeantasay (sic), Southside Johnny? Isn't R'n'B meant to be dead as an art form in nouvelle vague circles?"

The full-page advert for *Rattus Norvegicus* placed in *New Musical Express* in April stated that the first 10,000 copies would come with a free single. The content was unspecified.

Rattus Norvegicus was reviewed in the *Sniffing Glue* fanzine in April; "Apart from the title this LP is easy to understand. The natural progression of a band like The Stranglers is to have a first album that sounds like this. *Rattus Norvegicus* shows all their styles and proves that their inclusion in the lists of "new wave" bands is bullshit. The Stranglers are doing stuff that could have been done in '68, '70 or '72. Progressive rock will always be around. They write great songs — 'Sometimes', 'Hanging Around',

'Grip' etc. and they make the best of them."

"This whole album is excellent but I don't know why *Sniffing Glue* is reviewing it. Yeah, I secretly like The Stranglers' album. It's no longer a secret, this band will be very successful. America will fall over them. The Stranglers are quaint. They sing about acne, rats, "getting laid", "the Mersey tunnel" etc. They're incredibly British, their type of humour comes from their British upbringing and from a couple of years touring, playing the pub circuit and generally taking the rough with the smooth."

"Their sound is original and they never fail to surprise with sound effects and interesting fills. The individual members all have styles of their own. Hugh Cornwell on guitar and vocals, Jean-Jacques Burnel on bass and vocals, Dave Greenfield on keyboards (vocals on 'Peasant In The Big Shitty') and Jet Black on percussion. Jean's bass is the killer, it forms the base for most songs. The voices are good, especially when the lyrics allow for Hugh's odd quirks (as in 'Peaches' when he makes lots of weird noises)."

"I thought that 'Down In The Sewer' could have been a lot better. The stage version is much more adventurous but it doesn't spoil the overall quality of the album. One moan — why didn't they put the free single tracks (limited edition of 10,000) on the album and leave off 'Grip' and 'London Lady' which came out as a single last month? Some kids ain't gonna hear the free single which is a bit of a fucker. I don't know who thought of that stupid "free single" idea anyway. It's still a great album."

That's a damn good point about the free single content; whoever made that decision, why were they happy to run the risk of letting limited edition material fade into obscurity? Maybe that's an easy question to ask now though considering that at the time, The Stranglers were at the start of their career and nobody knew how big they would become thereafter. It's funny how the reviewer almost seems to imply that their enjoyment of The Stranglers is something of a guilty pleasure. It just goes to show that the band wasn't quite in the same stream as the likes of the Sex Pistols; a band that is was probably considered more "cool" or "punk" or whatever to like.

Rattus Norvegicus was reviewed in *Ghast Up* fanzine in May; "This album is very predictable, it's very much an attempt at getting away from the new wave dub by trying to adopt just about any other image. Yeah, I really like it but it does threaten. It threatens that the next twelve-inch Stranglers offering is gonna have longer, drawn out tracks and less of them, or even a concept. The Stranglers write some good stuff of which 'Peaches', the new single and the one everyone's raving over, is just about my least favourite. Best cuts are 'Hanging Around', 'London Lady' (sigh), 'Goodbye Toulouse' and '(Get A) Grip (On Yourself)'. I don't think this album's psychedelic at all. I think it's more sleazy-French-nightlife-type imagery. I can just imagine Hugh Cornwell strolling down the Pigalle telling all the prostitutes to fuck off."

"The psychedelia bit probably started with the track 'Ugly'. Wasn't psych — whatever, the period when everyone and everything was made of love, peace and beauty, or at least the surreal imagery surrounding it, and not images of acne greatly exaggerated by the influences of (whisper) L.S.D? Or has the truth behind the hippy movement been uncovered at last? — another Stranglers first."

"'Down In The Sewer' is the most sensational track, 'cos it's strange. I don't fancy living in a sewer, it's bad enough up here. The Stranglers have got an original sound, difficult to define. Dave Greenfield's organ playing, although overemphasised, does add that vital spark to the overall effect. It's commercial but not overtly. It grows on you, like 'Peaches'!"

As far as BBC airplay went, John Peel was in the minority of supporters in that regard. Whilst he played The Stranglers' music regularly, the other DJs didn't. Notably, it wasn't through the singles that The Stranglers got their exposure in 1977. As Burnel advocated at the time, it seemed to be The Stranglers' albums that people went for.

Rattus Norvegicus was reviewed in *Melody Maker* in April; "Just about the only predictable thing about rock is that as soon as something new comes along, there's always someone willing to jump on the band wagon. Even more predictable is that punk rock/new wave is going to get more than its fair share of these jerks, simply because it is a genre without rules and regulations."

"The Stranglers strike me as one such group attempting to cash in. On the face of it, they've got all the punk credentials – the name, the musical incompetence, even a gig supporting Patti Smith. But one look at this album is enough to let you know where The Stranglers are at – or perhaps, where their record company would like them to be at."

"There's a beautifully designed sleeve and inner sleeve, a special label with The Stranglers' rat logo and even – try and hide the groans – a free single. ELP should be so lucky! A special bonus for us lucky reviewers, there's a bundle of press cuttings, fax, pix and info, a press release that's magnificently mistyped and – here comes the real killer – a card from their *press and public relations consultant*. This is the music of disaffected youth, struggling against a hard business that won't give them a break? Smells more like hype to me."

"The music on the album confirmed that The Stranglers have little or nothing to offer. They're singularly lacking in all of the virtues that new wave bands like The Clash,

The Damned and the Pistols have as their saving grace — they're about as energetic as a slug, and their lyrics, far from providing an outlet for the frustrations of today's young, are the same old tripe used by most of the bands the punks love to hate — but with a few naughty swear words thrown in."

"Here's an example of the wit and wisdom of The Stranglers, from 'Peaches' — 'Strolling along, minding my own business, well there goes a girl now...'. All this is delivered in the usual arrogant tone, as though it were something momentous, and over a stunningly boring keyboard dominated riff. It has been suggested that The Stranglers resemble The Doors — an insult if ever I heard one. It's true that the opening cut, 'Sometimes', sounds like it's based on the 'Light My Fire' organ solo, yet they are more akin to a late sixties Detroit band, SRC, through their use of keyboards, but without half the Americans' style for exploiting doom-laden chords, nor even anything as remotely cheeky as combining 'Hall Of The Mountain King' with 'Beck's Bolero'."

"In truth, The Stranglers are no more than a cut-rate version of sixties American punk bands, but with none of the fizz that made that music so enjoyable. About the only thing they do well is write the titles to their songs — 'Grip', 'Down In The Sewer' and 'Ugly' promise something more interesting than a succession of deadening riffs and a noticeable lack of ideas. The only sense in which The Stranglers could be considered new wave is that no one has had the gall to palm off this rubbish before."

Whilst some reviews such as this were scathing, others were more positive, such as the one in *Record Mirror*; "How three blind mice musicians are led Indian file style into a drainy abyss by the loneliness in — such — a — drag voice of Hugh Cornwell. Hot rats in every way. See, The

Stranglers have this cold cream foundation of sound with Cornwell's stormtrooper tones pushing through the white mass like a sore. He's the street corner spiv with a suitcase, whispering in your ear, 'I've got something 'ere that might interest you' – viz 'Peaches', a package holiday song."

"But what really sets them apart from other new wave bands is Dave Greenfield's slicing keyboard work – 'Sometimes', 'Goodbye Toulouse' with its Pink Floyd 'Welcome To The Machine' fadeout and 'Grip', the single. Hence a Velvet Underground with balls tag – an understatement. Bassist Jean-Jacques Burnel, noted for his rodent-like stage movements, has a pretty fair voice himself, exemplified on 'London Lady', and Jet Black is a powerhouse drummer."

"Cornwell's guitar work occasionally sounds like Television's Tom Verlaine – on 'Princess Of The Streets', the best track on the initial hearing, and 'Hanging Around' – and that can't be bad. Oh and the final 'Down In The Sewer' suite, always effective live, comes off well on vinyl. Criticism? Shoddy production on one or two tracks and the annoying inclusion of a "limited edition" single, one side of which was recorded live at the Nashville. But apart from that, five stars."

Under the heading of "Women are strange when you're a Strangler", *Rattus Norvegicus* was reviewed in *New Musical Express* in April; "Evidently, the niceties of the late sixties social humanism – woman's lib, gay lib, and the respectful terminology that seemed such an essential basis for their fragile advances (not calling women "peaches" or gays "faggots" like you don't call blacks "nignogs" unless you're wearing a National Front armband and have crowd of thugs around you) – all this seems to have gone by the board with the emergence of a generation seemingly devoid of self-respect and thus, by trite by true extension, devoid of self-respect for others."

"It is with the defiantly oafish and thoughtlessly rebellious "attitude" that The Stranglers, visitors from another generation which may have wavered into complacency these past few years, choose to align themselves. Not being a great C&W fan, I'd have to think hard before I could name an album as grossly sexist as this. If I've misunderstood, and someone can demonstrate the underlying "subversiveness" of the insults that fly relentlessly at the opposite sex on *Rattus Norgevigus*, then I'll be overjoyed to understand, and to take back my criticisms. But don't tell me it's just The Rolling Stones and 'Brown Sugar' however many years on, because that was pretty pathetic too."

"Permanent immaturity is a heavy price for rock to pay for permanent youth, and maybe we're the ones who are afraid of change if we're prepared to pay that price. This is an album that can move people to tears — female people to tears of humiliation, that is. I've seen it happen. Really. Bully for The Stranglers — hey, they get a *real* response, those guys. They can make you feel sick too. Take it away boys. 'Some day I'm gonna smack your face...' That's 'Sometimes'. What is it? Realism? It's a godawful, vindictive reality in The Stranglers' minds then."

"Documentary? If so, it fails. If they are role playing then they're just a little too convincing. 'Little Lady, with Dingwalls bullshit, you're so stupid...' Jean-Jacques Burnel once actually quoted those words at me in order to show me 'London Lady' wasn't sexist, which is pretty extraordinary as it's a nauseating putdown of female promiscuity, with all the old, subliminal, reactionary what's-right-for-the-man-is-wrong-for-the-woman dogma whose destruction would prove a far more radical step than destroying tower blocks — a "policy" which The Stranglers, who actually once claimed to be "too political" for my taste, don't even advocate anyway."

The review continued; "Burnel's defence of his putdown of the Dingwalls groupie is that 'that's no way for a chick to be.' No way for a *what* to be? Go on JJ – 'We were drawing lots on who was going to screw this female column writer, and someone said, 'but it'd be like chucking a sausage up the Mersey Tunnel.' Someone else said 'Dangling a piece of string in a bucket.' It's been done before so we decided it wasn't valid to do it. It's just about some chicks in a very small scene. It's not a retrogressively sexist song,' he conceded, quoting a phrase from a previous review of mine."

"Well, you could fool me. For a start, without announcing before playing it that it's only about one person, not "London ladies" in general, it's bound to be taken as a generalisation, and how anyone who stands around sneering at a woman in such gross chauvinist terms can deny regressive sexism is quite beyond me. 'She's gone and left me, I don't know why, she's the queen of the street...' And he doesn't know why she left him. That's 'Princess Of The Streets'. The rest of it is a tribute to this "piece of meat's" animalistic (read less than human) sexuality."

"'Strolling along minding my own business...' That's 'Peaches'. The Stranglers patrol the beaches looking at the sex objects... It's demeaning just to listen to it. 'I was here, she was here, we did the only thing possible.' That's 'Ugly'. I don't think they talked about Heidegger, do you? There's only one thing "chicks" are good for eh? (yes I know insults like "chick" and "yummies" are horribly frequent in this paper – if I were you I'd write about it). 'I guess I shouldn't have strangled her to death...' Ah, the surrealist bit. Actually, he strangles her because her acne presumes massive proportions while she's tripping. Not the unreasonable moral of the story, which Burnel rather over-stresses by bellowing it out all unaccompanied is 'only the children of the fucking wealthy can afford to be good looking.' For once the grossness is in context as they end with JJ yelling 'muscle power, muscle power' but compared to The Clash's lyrics, this album is drivel."

"There might be some kind of justification if it were mixed with a vestige of the humanity which, as Nick Kent pointed out about The Clash, identifying it as 'a sense of morality', it's conspicuous by its absence from this scene. There might even be some justification if The Stranglers' sexism were tempered with the least iota of political drive. But their "political stance" is just that — a stance and nothing more, on the evidence of the songs."

"And the only thing they are is anti-women. Sad thing is, the joke's on us because this album is just so damn brilliant musically. The most playable record I've heard in ages, virtually every track is a little masterpiece. There isn't another new wave band within several leagues. Not that The Stranglers are astounding technicians — sure, they are compared with their peers, but follow them with a Bobby Womack LP (first in pile, is all) and their efforts might sound stilted. What The Stranglers have is the aggression that's today's currency, particularly Burnel's snapping bass, and a knack of stringing together great series of melodic, compelling riffs."

Still from the same review: "'Down In The Sewer' is the archetype, launching from a glorious warm peak into the riff that best conjures up Burnel and Hugh Cornwell's great patented sneakered Groucho walk, seesawing like some inane grin, before building to that weird sub-Ventures bubblegum psychedelic lick from Cornwell's twangy guitar. As Cornwell (a far better singer than JJ) spits out his crazy tale of life in the sewer, the band seethe monotonously behind him, Dave Greenfield rippling off into genuine archaic strangeness on his organ. And so on – an ever-shifting, disciplined, tough version of the darker psychedelic days (the strange ones, sure), perfectly arranged in a blunt, linear fashion – no coming back and finishing where you started for these blokes, once you've hammered a riff forget it – that rings weird and very refreshing."

"Tangible music with just the right immediacy on Martin Rushent's production... The Stranglers have somehow managed to find a place in rock that hasn't been overkilled, that is instantly comprehensible, yet is totally absorbing. The same claim could possibly be made for a handful of other recent arrivals, here and in the States, but for nobody can it be stated as strongly as for The Stranglers. And they do have good songs too. 'Hanging Around' and 'Goodbye Toulouse' and 'Grip' all have words that at least do not detract from (and with 'Hanging Around' positively enhance) the music which flows so splendidly throughout the album."

"The cloud nine lizard propulsion of 'Sometimes' drags you in, those twisty guitar/organ lines cushioning it so well and the chords soaring and skydiving. 'Toulouse' is a ridiculously thundering 3/4, like an army running as they re-envision Nostradamus' prophecy of the city's destruction. The subsequent Velvets bludgeoning and less than inspired individual shots of 'London Lady' are a let down. 'Princess Of The Streets' is amazing, a deliberate (as in robotic) Scots jig-meets-the-underworld, with sinuously wild-eyed, real lead guitar played real good by Cornwell As for 'Hanging Around', well it's just truly wonderful. 'He's alright in the city 'cause he's high above the ground...' Why can't they keep to that standard elsewhere? Anyway, it's a gas musically."

"Flipping, we get 'Peaches' — a really *violent* riff devalued by the wanky would-be Charles Atlas lyrical posturing until finally a really good line comes up, 'Oh shit, there goes the charabanc...' and for a few bars the riff changes completely, vanishing and coming in backwards like stubbing its toe. Great. 'Grip' is the single (next one's probably 'Go Buddy Go', which explains its absence), chugs along okay. 'Ugly' is, I think, Burnel's only vocal part apart from 'London Lady', and that's not the only reason they're the worst tracks — it's a noise and finally the ecstatic look-at-me-I'm-a-bad-guy *West Side Story* underground saga of 'Down In The Sewer'. A big tick for the music, an emphatic cross for the words — but words don't sell records. Perhaps sadly, they don't stop people buying either."

Wow! This was probably the most comprehensive and exploratory review done of *Rattus Norvegicus* at the time of its release. It's interesting how the reviewer (for what it's worth, Phil McNeill) felt that there was such a juxtaposition between the quality of the album's lyrics against the quality of the music. I advocate that this raises a question: "if the record contained exactly the same music but with completely different lyrics covering inoffensive topics, would *Rattus Norvegcius* have been the same album in terms of its overall character?" Probably not. That is to say that if it really was the case that the music was better than the lyrics, would it have really been possible to have had one without the other considering The Stranglers' overall image and if you will, brand?

Also (I promise not to go too deep into this as I appreciate that it is a divisive subject that will always mean different things to different people and to a passionate extent too), in terms of the sociological areas that the interview touches upon, it is clearly the case that for some branches of feminism (because indeed there are several that conflict with each other), The Stranglers' debut album was considered to be sexist. Well, maybe it was, maybe it wasn't but overall, it does raise the question of whether or not lyrics need to be taken as a moralistic message/ideology or are they simply, just something that is there to be taken at face value and as a tongue in cheek bit of fun.

It's such a subjective area and everyone will have their own bias on the topic but overall, I think it would have been a real shame for the musical output of The Stranglers to have been overlooked on the basis that some found the lyrics offensive.

A positive point of the *New Musical Express* review is that at least the reviewer is stringent in making a distinction between the fact that it's not the music that they have a problem with. I have no doubt that the quality of The Stranglers' music may have been overlooked on many occasions on the basis that to many, their lyrics were not considered appropriate.

Where the reviewer stipulates that they prefer Cornwell's vocals to Burnel's, well it's an interesting opinion but one that could be debated for eternity. Both vocalists brought a lot of power, emotion and character to a song and on such basis, The Stranglers' music would have been poorer without what both of them brought to the table as vocalists.

Perhaps reviews were never destined to be the be all and end all for The Stranglers anyway. Cornwell was quoted in *Record Mirror* in January; "I take all the music papers with a large pinch of salt. I find them far too heavily opinionated, more intent on saying what they want. The style has become more important than content. They are dealing with music which is an escape clause from the contract of life. The papers are existing in their own ivory towers. They don't have to struggle for stories, because they are always there. *Melody Maker* – it's got no humour, takes itself far too seriously. NME – the direct opposite, but just as bad. I've had a few bad experiences with them. I think you can distil the whole thing down to one reporter. The rest are probably old hippies. *Sounds* – always liked it because it treats new bands and established bands in the same way. *Rockstar* – Caters for the weenyboppers. I've read more coherent things in *Record Mirror. Record Mirror* – Find it quite refreshing. Contains articles on totally different things, which is very healthy. The papers don't always cite the truth. I reckon stories are far too heavily tampered with during the process from writing to printing."

It was reported in the *Daily Mirror* in July that The Stranglers had "been together for two years. Their album *Rattus Norvegicus* jumped from number sixteen to number four within a week and has already passed the 100,000 mark, having sold 30,000 copies within three days of release. Their second single, 'Peaches', is still in the charts and has sold 100,000 copies. One of the few British punk bands to get an American record deal."

Although they didn't seem to have their hearts set on America, efforts to engage were still made by some of the band. Black was quoted in *Record Mirror* in August; "Hugh's already over there, on holiday. We'll be going round doing the radio stations, giving interviews. It'll be hard work. I hope the flight's alright. I don't like flying, I like to have my feet firmly on the ground. Anyway, the album's been released over there and it's getting radio airplay. One New York station is playing several tracks and in Los Angeles they're playing complete sides. It's looking good. I don't think we've got any plans for single releases over there yet."

More evidence that the band's debut made a strong impact not long after it was released comes from a report in *Record Mirror* in July: "The Stranglers became the first of the new wave bands to get a silver disc this week for sales of their first album, *Rattus Norvegicus* for £150,000 (worth of) sales."

Endearingly and true to their word, with their debut album, The band had stuck to their original remit. Jet Black told *Zigzag* in November 1976; "We wanted to do our kind of music, which is a beat off-beat when one looks at current trends. We didn't want to follow everybody else and we have stuck to that. In the early days the criticism was pretty horrendous! Now people realise we are refreshingly different and that's what we wanna stick to... We're not really aware of influences, but people say we're influenced by The Doors and Velvets. We don't know. We listen to all sorts of music."

To which Cornwell was quoted, "Jean and I were at college for three years between 1968 and 1972. You know when you're at college you get introduced to a lot of new sounds. We got influenced by what we heard in that period. All that time we were absorbing things and not really knowing how they were going to come out. I dunno if you've noticed, but absolutely fuck all's happened since about 1970 when Hendrix died. A couple of bands split up and a few people died but really nothing's happened. Everything's been like a throw-over from those times. It's all coming out a bit later."

In some ways, success was perhaps a double-edged sword. Burnel recalled in *The Quietus* in March 2014; "We started getting ostracised by all the people we thought were our mates, the press started taking sides and started to slag us off. Of course, when our first album, *Rattus Norvegicus*, came out, we outsold everyone and they were really cheesed off. So we'd start hearing things like, 'They use keyboards so they can't be a part of this and they're using synthesisers so they're definitely not a part of this new thing' and that kind of stuck. But it was good for us because it meant that we didn't have to subscribe to any new orthodoxies or new forms of fundamentalism and we could do what we want... We just allowed ourselves to follow our musical noses. We weren't straight-jacketed by expectations. I remember on the first album there's a 6/8 waltz on it and there's stuff that's prog rock, really, like 'Down In The Sewer' and it was full of everything that inspired us in the first place. When you're a young band, your first album usually reflects your obvious influences and you find your own identity later on."

The originality of *Rattus Norvegicus* was such that it opened more doors for The Stranglers. Not only that but musically, it's a damn good album.

Performing at The Roundhouse. The band played there several times in 1977.

Posing for the press before the gig at Wolverhampton, 31st May.
L-R Dave Greenfield, Jet Black, Hugh Cornwell,
Jean-Jacques Burnel.

Electric Circus, Manchester, 5th June. J.J. still managed to play the
gig with his hand heavily bandaged.

Posing for a photo in Manchester prior to their gig at the Electric Circus on 5th June. Burnel's hand is heavily bandaged, apparently from an injury sustained at the Wigan Casino the previous night.

At the Electric Circus, Manchester, 5th June.
This picture captures the rawness of The Stranglers' early gigs.

21st September 1977. L-R: Jet Black, Hugh Cornwell, Jean-Jacques Burnel and Dave Greenfield. Despite the band's reputation they made for good headlines so photo shoots for the press were a common occurrence.

Crawley Sports Centre, 30th September 1977.

The Locarno Ballroom, Coventry, 4th October 1977

The Locarno Ballroom, Coventry, 4th October 1977

The last gigs of the year were in Amsterdam. Whilst in the
Netherlands they also appeared on the Dutch TV show *Top Pop*
miming to 'No More Heroes'.

Given the miming scenario, there was also a take where they joked about on each other's instruments.

Chapter Three

No More Heroes

Even at the time, record labels were concerned that punk would fizzle out in Britain as quickly as it had arrived. Regarding the popularity of punk and new wave, Cornwell told the *Aberdeen Evening Express* in December; "The whole thing will take about five years and then it will be someone else's turn."

The management also had concerns that The Stranglers would self destruct. As a result, in June it made sense for United Artists to get them back into the studio to make a second album. Several tracks had already been done during the sessions for *Rattus Norvegicus*; only a few more numbers were needed for what would become *No More Heroes* as the record company insisted in around forty minutes in total, the ideal length for a vinyl album.

Notably, although they both contain a different number of tracks, both *Rattus Norvegicus* and *No More Heroes* are around this length. Maybe some had more confidence in the longevity of The Stranglers' music than others. In terms of the direction he anticipated new wave and punk going in and whether it would last, Black was quoted in *Record Mirror* in August; "I think it will — when the history of pop music is written — be an important era. Some of the bands are going to be very big, like the Sex Pistols."

In September, journalist Chas De Whalley writing in *Sounds* described what it was like being in the studio with The Stranglers as they worked on their second album. He reported that overall, there was a friendly and relaxed atmosphere in the studio, at least for The Stranglers; they were familiar with the studio and their material, so much so that they were jaunty and jovial as they worked.

Producer Martin Rushent, on the other hand, appeared stressed and exasperated as he chain-smoked at the mixing desk. In fairness though, Burnel was messing about on the drums when it was Greenfield's turn to record a take. Although Rushent could see the funny side, he apparently said to Burnel, "That's great JJ. If you really want drum spill all over the track, you're doing a really great job."

Greenfield got a bit irritated in the moment because he wanted to get on with recording but overall, it was reported that that morale and energy was good across the board with everyone.

'Peasant In The Big Shitty', 'School Mam', 'Something Better Change' and 'Bitching' had already been recorded. Burnel was quoted in *Strangled* from an interview that took place in May; "We have been laying down tracks when we have felt right about them. It hasn't been a case of saying 'right, this block of time, this week, nine 'til five we will record the new LP'."

"For *Rattus*, it was different. We had a set to record. A lot of the next LP was also done then. We don't play many of the songs on *Rattus* live anymore because when you write a song, the gap between the time you write it and then play it is the credibility gap. The longer the gap, the less relevant it is to you... We have more relevant statements to make. I don't like promoting an LP just for the sake of it. If people don't like our set because half the numbers are not on the LP, too bad. We could easily just go out to promote the LP and a lot of people would like that. It's the first time that we have had a really large audience, whereas before it was small groups of friends.

It was very close, you know, down at the Nashville etc. So now if people are dissatisfied because we don't play all of the LP, too bad. We have never wanted to compromise."
'Burning Up Time' and 'English Towns' were written for the new album. Overall, a lot of the writing had been done much earlier on. In January, *Sideburns* listed songs that had appeared as part of a live set in late 1976; 'Straighten Out', 'London Lady', 'Something Better Change', 'Goodbye Toulouse', 'Peaches' and 'Go Buddy Go'.

Also, It was reported in *Zigzag* in November 1976; "Over the last year the band has steadily built up its large following with explosive sets including such classic tunes as 'Go Buddy Go', 'Bitching', 'Down In The Sewer', 'Peasant In The Big Shitty', 'School Mam', 'Tomorrow As The Hereafter' and 'Mean To Me'. They've hung onto 'Walk On By' from the old days 'cos it's evolved into something astoundingly different from Burt's original... All the band writes the music and the lyrics are written by 'Whoever's got the most to grouse about at the time. These are based on experience but a few are fantasised'."

"At the moment the group's songwriting is prolific but an intense gig schedule means they don't get much time to work up the new stuff. The Stranglers openly admit that 'strange things outside of the music' help shape the strong, often disturbing songs. They won't be drawn into revealing these "strange things" though. When pressed in best News-Of-The-World-shock-probe fashion, an offended Hugh exclaimed, 'But that's our private lives! It's got nothing to do with the general public'."

One of the most striking things about The Stranglers compared to other bands regarded as punk in 1977, was the predominance of Dave Greenfield's keyboard contribution. Those, combined with Burnel's demanding bass lines were a key feature of The Stranglers' sound and this is very much apparent in the opening track, 'I Feel Like A Wog'. The keyboard riff pushes the song along in a way that is unrelenting and it functions as an excellent background in support of Cornwell's growling vocals.

Cornwell told *Record Mirror* in September; "The album is an advancement. We've used synthesiser on four or five tracks, we're using it onstage now as well. It's given dimension and some ideas too — about structure of the songs... The synthesiser's sparked us into a new field. We still write songs but that's because we want people to tell us whether we've still got a song there. We've changed a lot of basic things about the song, the structure, the fitting of lyrics to music, the timing and things like that. And if it's a success we'll develop that more on the next album. We want to explore new territory, instead of writing pretty little songs for the next ten years. We could do that quite easily, but we want to explore, we want to learn too. Synthesisers up until now have been associated with psychedelic, heady music that has no direction. We want to give it direction."

Despite the controversial use of the word Wog, 'I Feel Like A Wog' is in empathy of the alienation that immigrants and other outsiders may feel. It was written not long after *Rattus Norvegicus* has been released. Cornwell speaking to *Record Mirror* said; "We met this guy in Hamburg called Pimpo, and he was a pimp. He thought we were a big band at that time, which we weren't and we kidded him that we were this other band so that he would sell us some women. In the end he was getting really worried because he couldn't work out who we were, and he was annoyed because this other band hadn't turned out. He had all these women lined up and he wouldn't give them to us because we had no money. So I tried to tell him some jokes to cheer him up and he didn't understand them. He just kept asking questions about things that had happened earlier in the joke. He looked at me like I was really strange, like I was a foreigner, and I felt really alien, like a wog, you know. The word wog was introduced to distinguish certain people from other people, and I started thinking about how people are made to feel the same way. Alienation."

Burnel added; "I've been a wog all my life. My parents are French. At school I was treated like a wog, because my mother used to kiss me at the school gates and I had shorts as well — really short. It used to freak me out, because I wanted to be more English than the English. Then I realised, this is crazy, you know, I might as well be who I am. It wasn't too bad for me because I am white, and it was only people who knew we were French, it was only at school. It still hassled me though — so God knows how black people feel sometimes."

Burnel told *Shews*; "When we were In Germany they made us feel like wogs. It also says what a real drag it is for coloured people or anyone else for that matter who people might look at when they're walking down the street, and make out as if they're aliens, just because of the colour of their skin. That's the kind of ignorance we're trying to fight. It's a very energetic number."

He expanded further on the subject to *New Musical Express* in October; "I used to get beat up every day at school in Guildford, because I'm French — both my parents are French but I was born in Notting Hill Gate. So because I was *different*, because I was *French*, I couldn't make friends and I was always getting beaten up. So by the time I was seventeen, I was a *Nazi*."

Burnel was kicked out of school for this. He was quoted in the same feature, "That's when I lost interest in all that bullshit and took up karate. I've got a brown belt now. I was seventeen and very resentful and no one was ever going to push me around again... Everyone should be multinational. I have both British and French passports."

An endearing aspect of 'Bitching' is in how as soon as the song opens, it showcases all of the instruments in The Stranglers' ensemble. Burnel contributed the vocals to this track. The guitar solo that takes place during the bridge of the song is particularly memorable. When Cornwell came up with the music for the song, it was his intention to create something that had a strong groove to it à la Velvet Underground's 'Sweet Jane'.

Lyrically the song makes reference to The Stranglers' friendship with the Hell's Angels and there is also a whole verse dedicated to the time when the band hired out their PA in Peckham. Cornwell told *Record Mirror* in September; "The lyrics of 'Bitching' are Jean's. The song is just about grousing about the tin gods we met when we were struggling to get gigs."

Burnel added; "We came in on the tail end, the very tail end of the pub scene, and we started gigging around. It was difficult for us to get jobs on that scene, because we had short hair and didn't play the sort of music that was accepted. We didn't know anyone, we didn't get introduced to anyone. We weren't part of it, we were by ourselves. I also found that the promoters just didn't know what they were talking about, and they treated us like dirt. The audiences were pretty bad sometimes — they were so narrow-minded in their attitudes. They couldn't understand us. So 'Bitching' is all about the shitheads we met."

Regarding what the lyrics were getting at, Jet Black said in *Sideburns* in January; "I guess you could say that we are trying to put across what we see as we live our lives. All our lyrics contain instances that have happened like 'Bitching' is relating to our first visit to Amsterdam and there are lots of people that we see that are in the lyrics."

'Dead Ringer' has a sinister sound to it whereby on vocals, Greenfield sings about how people feel the need to follow trends in order to belong and have a sense of validation. His voice is very crooner-like (he was a lead singer in another band prior to joining The Stranglers).

The bass line is not too different to the one that was used on 'Peaches', but it is a little faster. 'Dead Ringer' was written and recorded around the same time as 'I Feel Like A Wog' and 'In The Shadows'. All three of those songs feature chords that are more jazzy than some of the other Stranglers songs.

In later years, Cornwell noted that because 'Dead Ringer' had been written not long before it was recorded, it sounds fresh on the record. Burnel said in *Shews*; "A song is only valid during the time that you're writing it. So it's a bit of a cop out after you've written it. The next day, it's not so valid. But it's nice to have it on a mechanical form like a record or tape, so you can leave it there as it is, and not improve on it. We've put quite a few new songs on recently."

Speaking to *Record Mirror* in September he added; "'Dead Ringer''s about certain bands or certain people who say what they're about when they're not. Like people who say, 'Was it you who's proud of being poor' and they make big deal of it, because they know there's a market for it. Like the old wave bands have done it — I mean the old wave new wave. There's five main bands — the Pistols, The Clash, The Damned, The Jam and ourselves, and everyone's taking their examples from us, opinion and attitude wise. I'm very suspicious of motives. Now there's a lot of bands adopting stances that others have come to more naturally. Attitudes that they've adopted overnight. 'Dead Ringers''s about hypocrisy."

From Cornwell's perspective; "A dead ringer is someone who looks exactly like someone else, so it's about a few experiences we've had where we've asked people about things they've been quoted as saying and they go 'No. It wasn't me mate' Or you say, 'Didn't I see you doing that?' and they say no and the answer is they must be the spitting image of someone who did."

The spoken narrative that accompanies the music comes across as a thoughtful tribute to Dagenham Dave on the track named after him. The last verse of the song refers to the gig that took place at the 100 Club just before the Sex Pistols started their UK tour with The Clash. That night, Dave got in a fight with the Finchley Boys. It had an effect on him to the point that this event is largely attributed as a catalyst for Dave's suicide. In later years, Cornwell described the fight as "the worst thing I'd ever seen at one of our gigs."

Contemporaneously Cornwell told *Record Mirror* in September; "Dagenham Dave was this spade guy from Manchester who put an end to himself one night because — well, I don't know his motives, but I know he was very depressed with life. The only thing that pleased him was the fact that we were getting more popular. He came to all our gigs when we were first getting started last year. He was a scaffolder who'd done so many things. He'd been to a lot of places, lived through a lot of existences. He was thirty, and he just felt he'd had enough experiences for one life. In the end they dragged him out of the Thames after three weeks, just a bag of mush. He jumped off Tower Bridge."

Burnel was quoted in the same feature; "He was an amazing bloke. He lived in this hotel room for £25 a week with his old lady Brenda, and he was a maniac. He was such a genuine guy and he was so intelligent, but he'd just go bananas. He had this amazing collection of records which he never played – they were all in mint condition. He was a real rock 'n' roll hero. He used to earn a hundred quid a week, and one night he blew a hundred and twenty quid just on having a good time. He was broke the next week, but he didn't care – he didn't give damn. He was on 'Go Buddy Go'. The single was really poxy compared to other recordings of it that we've done since, but he just turned up that night and freaked out the whole studio, and we forgot about recording and just had a good time with Dagenham Dave. It just freaks me out to think that a guy I was so into killed himself. It's like an insult you know, because it's like he didn't believe we were there."

With The Stranglers having already been labelled as misogynistic, it is very possible that 'Bring On The Nubiles' was done as a wind up – that whole idea of playing up to people's hysteria in order to mock them for it. However, in later years Cornwell asserted that the song grew from the band simply getting carried away when jamming in the studio and wondering how much they could get away with in view of their higher profile by this point (something of a reaction to the fact that when they were starting out, they had had to learn standards like 'Tie A Yellow Ribbon' in order to comply with audience expectations).

When he wrote the lyrics for 'Bring On The Nubiles', Cornwell had not long read *Lolita* by Nabokov. In later years, he has stipulated that the song was "not meant to promote any activity whatsoever." As he explained at the time; "A nubile is a girl who personifies the innocence and charm of a flowering girl. They can be any age, but they have it, somehow. It's a song in praise of that. A lot of women become very jaded when they reach a certain age, so nubility is definitely not a thing that lasts. It's a transient thing. Men are like red wine – they get better with age. Girls are like white wine – they only taste good when drunk young. Maybe that's the quandary that girls always have and always will be in – what happens when they lose that quality. Maybe that's their sad fate."

Burnel's take on it was, "The Stranglers are the band to call sexist, aren't they? *Spare Rib* really put us down you know – I'm sure they're a load of dikes over there. That's a really clichéd attitude, but they're often the truest. Boots and W H Smiths were going to ban the album because of the lyrics on this track."

He told *New Musical Express* in October; "The trouble with women is that their bodies decline so quickly. By the time they're forty they're soft and flabby, whereas you see handsome men at forty."

'Something Better Change' has an anthem-like quality to it, particularly in how the anticipation builds at the start of the song with the organ prior to Burnel's loud grunt that leads into the distinctive riff.

An antagonistic song, it had been left over from the *Rattus Norvegicus* recording sessions. It was written even earlier in the summer of 1976. Regarding 'Something Better Change', Cornwell said; "It's just about attitudes." Burnel concurred; "It speaks for itself."

It was shortly after the release of the debut album that the title track of their second one began to take shape. The week before they wrote it, Both Elvis and Groucho Marx died and according to Cornwell in later years, it fuelled the idea of there being no more heroes. In fact, in bootlegs featuring earlier performances of the song, he sings "there's no more heroes so don't make any more."

However, the song isn't necessarily about the loss of heroes, so much so that The Stranglers went through a period of refusing to sign autographs on the basis that they felt people should be their own heroes and not look for it in others.

Cornwell told *Record Mirror*; "You should be your own hero. If you become a hero, people don't see you for what you are, they look at you in a different light. You cease to become human to them and that's wrong. There are two bad ways to treat a human being — you can either treat them like dirt or you can treat them so good that you're not treating them as human beings either. Human beings aren't gods. Having heroes is like a cop out. It's seeing something in someone else. But people should be striving to get that in themselves."

Regarding the concept of 'No More Heroes', Burnel said; "It's a slogan as well as a title. We try to live without the star system, and we succeed quite well, I think."

Ironically though, as Cornwell said; "We're up there singing 'No More Heroes' and in front of us are thousands of kids going crazy. It's almost as if we're perpetuating the very myth we set out to destroy."

The keyboard riff is memorable and so are the lyrics. Arguably one of The Stranglers' most iconic tracks to this day, 'No More Heroes' highlights how different they were in their use of keyboards.

In particular, 'No More Heroes' is immensely keyboard dominated to the extent that it is arguably one of the most memorable features of the song entirely — it gets in your head and it stays there! Not only that, but the keyboard part drives the song overall. 'No More Heroes' really is a masterpiece when taking into account the originality of the lyrics as they abruptly lament the passing of the likes of Trotsky, Lenin, Elmyra, Shakespeare and Sancho Panza.

Cornwell was quoted in *Strangled* in summer 1977; "I went to Trotsky's house and paid my respects... They have left all his stuff on the tables exactly as it was covered with a plastic sheet and it is going yellow. It is very weird.

And he is buried in the garden and I had a great sense of achievement just going there."

The 'No More Heroes' single was reviewed in *Sounds* in September; "Jean-Jacques Burnel tells me I can't review his new album 'cos I'll be too partisan. So gimme the single instead. 'Whatever Happened To The Heroes' (sic) isn't the best up for grabs on the LP but it's easily the strongest, loudest, classiest 45 in this week's bunch. Take Hugh Cornwell's tirade against the fragility of today's political and social figureheads and mate it with Iggy Pop/Syd Barrett nightmare dub jam on the other side and discover The Stranglers the most adventurous and imaginative band in the world on September 14th in this the year of Our Lord 1977. But you'll have to buy the single to get hold of that Barracuda Bass on the B-side — 'cos it won't be on any album."

Dave Greenfield contributes the vocals to 'Peasant In The Big Shitty'. It is interesting how the pleasantness of the guitar almost seems to be in juxtaposition to the driving and angry sounds of the bass and keyboards. The song is in 9/4 time and this was a key reason as to why Greenfield did the vocals for it; when Cornwell and Burnel tried to sing it, they struggled with the timing. Jet Black's drumming is phenomenal on this song. Playing in 9/4 is effectively like playing a bar of 4/4 and then a bar of 5/4 over and over again. It's not easy by any stretch.

Cornwell speaking to *Record Mirror* in September said; "It's about being a peasant, and it has very psychedelic lyrical patterns, where reality's doubted, and you don't know what's real any more. People sometimes aren't real. The city is London, because that was our big shitty."

Burnel added; "It's specifically about us being poor, and having just come to London. And besides that, being on acid."

For 'Burning Up Time', Burnel wrote the lyrics about taking a train to Brighton to see his girlfriend. The song was written quickly and is an exploration into hedonism. Cornwell explained; "It's about people wanting to utilise their time in the best possible way, because it's running out fast! Every minute counts. There was a guy who was in the army who took the most boring job, which was peeling potatoes because it made each moment last so long and he really enjoyed living."

Burnel added; "It's about not living safely, about doing everything as it comes to you. It's a speed song. You burn yourself up if you don't play safe."

'English Towns' was rarely played live. The reason for this was that the band regarded it as filler; it was something that they threw in towards the end of the sessions when everyone was tired from having given it their all. To say that the song was without meaning would be to do it a disservice though.

Cornwell said; "It's like a very sad feeling you sometimes get when you're very used up, and when you haven't had a good sexual feeling for a while. You find the feelings, but they're not the ones you really want 'No love in a thousand girls' is one of the lines in it, and 'The dogs try to posses us.' The dogs are the London ladies."

Burnel's take on the song was that it was "about love — love being debased or that there's no such thing. The word is thrown round much too easily. If there's too much love in the world, where is it? If there was more love about, people would stop ripping each other off and nations would be much more sensitive to other nations."

'School Mam' was originally going to be called 'School Man' but it developed into 'School Mam' as work continued on it. Cornwell wanted to create something that was similar to 'The Gift' by Velvet Underground in terms of how hypnotic it sounds. The mental maths section began its life as an adlib that Cornwell developed over time. The decision to speak rather than sing was based on him wanting to make the song sound as hypnotic as possible.

The drum part is very tom orientated. The sound effect of kids in the playground at the end of 'School Mam' was Martin Rushent's idea. Cornwell told *Record Mirror* in September; "That's a piece of dialogue about a situation in a school where the teacher calls one of the kids to stay behind and help after class and they start getting it on. The mistress who's in charge of the school has video screens in all the classrooms, and she sees what they're doing. And instead of calling the police, she starts watching it and getting off on it, and she ends up having an orgasm, which she's never had before in her life. She's about eighty, and she dies in front of the screen with a smile on her face. That's the best way to go, to die having an orgasm. It must be. I've never done it but it must be the way to go."

Burnel; "You know Hugh was kicked out of school for perverting the kids? He was kicked out of this tutorial collage for being a bad influence on kids, for being an undesirable."

Even with the social norms of the time taken into account, the latter does not make for comfortable reading. The fact that it was printed just a week before the album was released speaks volumes about the fact that with The Stranglers, when it came to letting people know what their songs were about, it was a case of "here it is, it's not nice but take it or leave it."

It's not surprising that some really hated The Stranglers but with a lyric like "stick my fingers straight up your nose" on 'Something Better Change', its not as if they were trying to sugar coat anything. 'School Mam' went down well at gigs and it was often during this number that Cornwell would pretend to masturbate his throat, a trick that he had been taught by a friend of his who had trained at drama school.

No More Heroes was reviewed in the *Daily Mirror* in September; "Powerful and slick with more than a touch of rawness that goes a long way to explain why The Stranglers are being recognised as one of the best new wave bands."

It was considered in *New Musical Express* in October; "The second album, *No More Heroes*, is the logical progression of the first, with more blood-stained pubic hair. It's performed with stunningly calculated miasma and although it takes no risks whatsoever and there's less that you'd want to whistle while shaving your legs – it's such a brilliant example of mass production product that in all probability it will still be showing on the album charts this time next year... The Stranglers' kind of rock music has replaced wars and football fields as the answer to macho sexual liberation." To which Cornwall was quoted, "Women like to be dominated. I think that subservient women are pitiful."

It was considered in *Sounds* in September; "Punk purists may knock The Stranglers for those operatic productions. They may even claim The Stranglers aren't even a new wave band at all and use that sound gushing from their speakers as evidence backing their case. Certain critics will doubtlessly brand the *No More Heroes* album 'another case of middle-class angst from those sexist hedonistic and existentialist Stranglers' but this is still a democracy and idiots are allowed their opinions."

"The Stranglers hearts are firmly with the "new politics" of rock even if they approach it from up the fire escape and criticise its back yard while supporting its façade. Already classic Stranglers numbers like 'I Feel Like A Wog',

'Dagenham Dave', 'No More Heroes' and 'Peasant In The Big Shitty' — all on the new album — are by no means songs of selfish appetite. They question the status quo as strongly as The Clash, and only 'Something Better Change' could be criticised as mere sloganry. They question the motives and the integrity of the revolutionaries too. 'Dead Ringer' quite shamelessly points the finger at some of the big punk politicians. But what about the X Certificate porn of 'School Mam' or the decadence of that brand new tune 'Bring On The Nubiles'? Our feminist friends won't buy those two, that's for sure. The Stranglers are ready to pull the sheets off anybody — *you* even — and if that doesn't give them new wave credibility then the boring old farts are right. The whole thing is nothing but a fashion."

No More Heroes was reviewed in *Sounds* in September (a different week to the former piece); "Ahhh, but these are testing times — now the very real euphoria has subsided, the scales have fallen from my eyes, not recantation, but re-evaluation. Timely sift and sort. Now I'm blinded I can really see. Oh, The Stranglers, such nice boys. But they *need* to be nasty, so squalid. And they do it so well. Look at Hugh Cornwell, standing on stage, posture saying 'C'mon man, c'man get me, g'wan, I dar ya.' They want to get up your nose. They want to shock. They want to confront you with the seamy white underbelly. Okay, okay, okay."

"So why did *Rattus Norvegicus* sell so well then? Because they're bright and talented enough to translate their aggression and studied venom into direct musical terms — an instantly recognisable sound (which'll be hard to break away from) that scrapes under your skin and lodges there, even better as an irritant. You can't escape it. And of course they're heavy metal macho cross-over — perfect for the time when there wasn't much punk product and most were unconverted but curious."

"And it was brilliantly produced, and their constant playing paid dividends, and it was right in there with the then zeitgeist – all that stuff about rats and angry, suitably "change" oriented lyrix (sic). Well here we are with new product, all tarted up in a hideous – successful indeed as kitsch – chintzy chocolate-box style sleeve. Inside, on cue, a rat appears – very reassuring. The themes of utter negativity, seediness, sleazo inputs continue, only, by the great law of Alice Cooper, a little more hysterical, more strident, just nastier. Oh look – more titles for "liberals" to get fussed about – 'I Feel Like A Wog', 'Bring On The Nubiles' and some creepy-crawlies. 'Mam' – the rest of the band meshes so closely that his voice is given more prominence. Under close scrutiny, it seems forced, trying to be tough, macho, too hard."

"And the subject matter, 'Wog', 'Nubiles', 'Bitching' – point taken. Holding up a mirror, confrontation etc. (although 'Nubiles' comes over most as being adolescent) – but who needs them as moralisers? Agreed that having your face rubbed in a cesspit can, on certain occasions, be salutary (shock/emetic). Beyond a point, reached on this album, it seems more redundant, self-indulgent. I mean we know already that England's "going down the toilet", we've been told often enough. What to *do* about it? Because The Stranglers offer nothing positive, not even in their music. Look, the Pistols tell you we're being flushed too, but their music has a kick, a bounce, a tension that gives you energy, makes you want to do something. Some sort of life out of decay. 'Peasant In The Big Shitty', 'School Mam'. Sort of like *Plague Of The Zombies*."

The review continued; "Oh you guessed, I don't like the album. I've tried very hard (really, for all the "right" reasons) but I still think it sucks. No, this isn't a critic's set-em-up-and-shoot-em-down exercise, nor a virulent manifestation of putative new wave elitism. The Stranglers convinced me they had something when I heard 'Grip' thundering out over Portobello Road and couldn't rest until I'd found out who it was. I've got no axe to grind, but what I hear now turns me right off. It'll sell. Half the album is full of very strong material — songs with are ridiculously catchy and well constructed and, oh yeah, they stay in the head — 'No More Heroes', 'Dagenham Dave', 'Bitching' and the best, 'Burning Up Time'. The rhythm section is simply very tight, relentless, while the organ that fleshes the sound out (and *does* bring to mind Seeds/Doors at 45 comparisons) holds some kind of magical power with its hypnotic swell, sinister undertone."

"Oh yes, they can do it. But it sounds so *assembled* somehow. And the material isn't as consistent as last time around. Some of the songs, 'Dead Ringer', 'School Mam', 'Peasant In The Big Shitty' are plain awkward, embarrassing in parts. A problem is Cornwell's lyrix/stance, and the band's intrinsic and deep coldness. No amount of "intellectual" rationalisation can get round the fact that too many lyrix are dumb. Dumb — and Cornwell patently isn't. Like at the end of 'Burning Up Time' he goes into this 'hello little girl, want a sweetie' routine, and blows it. 'Bitching', with its 'why don't you all go get screwed' refrain. Or the platitudes of 'Something Better Change'. Or the end of 'School Mam'. The Stranglers rumble along relentlessly, zombied, with sledgehammer blows driving their message home. They move, but they can be so wooden. Like a skimming coffin lid."

"I suppose they got up my nose, didn't they? So they win in the end. Some pyrrhic victory though. The music's powerful enough to get some reaction (always better than none) but what comes off this album, with its deliberate unrelenting wallowing, is the chill of death. No life force, nothing vital. Not so that it's frightening, just dull and irritating, ultimately. And it doesn't make it as a statement, even though it's all taken so seriously. Oh well, you can take it or leave it. They need this review like a hole in the head, so do you — no doubt you'll buy it anyway. I know it isn't aimed at me, but it sounds as though everyone's intelligence is being insulted, yours, mine, and that of this record's creators."

Blah blah, moan moan. It sounds like the reviewer got out of the wrong side of bed that day. Was he not blown away the first time he heard 'No More Heroes' open side two of the LP?! For most Stranglers fans, I would imagine that the above review is difficult to digest because it doesn't say anything positive about the music that has become such a point of enjoyment for so many people. On balance though, the review is important because it is reflective of what The Stranglers were up against in 1977 in terms of those who found their music offensive or perhaps simply, just not to their taste.

I advocate that the following is the best review of *No More Heroes*, not just because it favours a positive fan bias, but on the basis that it was one of the few reviews that endeavoured to comment on the music more than The Stranglers' public image. The review basically ignores the bollocks and focuses on the music which, after all, is the very thing that determines a lasting legacy of any band.

The beauty of fanzines — in terms of how those who wrote for them were more often interested in what mattered rather than what is now often referred to as "celebrity gossip". Notably, the review also makes reference to what the original intentions were for the cover art of *No More Heroes*. So yeah, here it is, the review of *No More Heroes* from *Strangled*;

"The time has come again for me to do an over the

top review of the new LP. I will try to keep my head on. Okay? It has now been one year since The Stranglers were gigging in London at the Red Cow, Nashville, and the Hope and Anchor every night of the week. Since that time they have had their first LP out, they have acquired a lot of pseudo friends and neighbours who want to be invited to the next kebab evening when the new LP comes out. The last laugh is on them. Everyone knows who these turds are. So lig off. Also, some people have actually written to me saying things like 'Of course I used to live in Finchley' or 'I know some people from Finchley.' What is the game? All propaganda."

"True to their word, the lads have not suddenly decided to do the Hammersmith Odeon circuit. They remain in control. And now they have this new LP out, just as amazing as the first one. It is more viscous I think, harder. There is a sense of anger — we will not compromise. A lot of the numbers you will be familiar with, a few not so, also the more familiar numbers sound great captured at last. By the time you have heard the record and maybe gone to see them, yet more new numbers will have started to come out, and that will be their third LP!"

"I haven't got the cover of the LP yet but what I have seen has JJ on Trotsky's tomb. Not his real one you dork! Anyway, this is it. Side one, 'I Feel Like A Wog' — not as that turd on the evening or something or other paper said (is) a reggae number, as we all know. This is superb. As usual you have JJ's throbbing bass — sorry girls — with Hugh pleading his story, 'he didn't get the joke and then he made me feel like a wog.' It happens every fucking day of the week. This puts it all into words in an almost desperate way. Don't call me a golliwog! Now and then Hugh's voice turns into an echo and disappears into a power chord."

The review continued; "'Bitching' — one of the old faves

from way back when, (a) really great riff all the way through. JJ on voice. Jet once said to me that it concerned incidents that happened to them when they went to Amsterdam last year. Hugh contributes a really great twangy guitar. As ever, Jet and Dave are there. 'Why don't you all go and get screwed. Why don't you tell me something new?' 'Dead Ringer' – a new song that opens with JJ on bass and Jet just tapping a cymbal. The whole song then just explodes. I think it is Dave on vocals on this one, singing in a jazzy style, with Dave's usual Dr Phibes overtones. I have never seen Dave's shadow so I'm pretty sure that he is a vampire anyway so this would seem to ring true from his voice."

"The music continues and then shudders to a stop. 'Productivity,' he shouts, 'credibility,' 'profitability.' The song final catapults into a stop. 'Dagenham Dave' – one of The Stranglers' mates who only six months ago was dancing on stage with them at the Roxy. A very personal song to the band. We have heard it before on stage. JJ does the vocals which develops into a brief talking over music. Dave's keyboards twist and turn like the waves. It happened."

"'Bring On The Nubiles' – really creepy and violent. A love song, says Hugh. Ban it, says the Smiths, Woolworths etc. of the world. Dave uses a Moog on this. Hugh is on the voice, the whole riff has a Kinks type flavour to it. Dave really gets some weird sounds from this Moog. As good as Eno on the first Roxy LP. Just as original, it all ends dead."

"'Something Better Change' – the most recent single sung by JJ, we all know this one 'Stick my fingers right up your nose,' Hugh again does a crashing guitar solo. 'No More Heroes' – another great song, sung by Hugh. These heroes are Trotsky, Lenin, they are all dead. Dave seems to supply the main riff in this and in the middle section is Dave, Jet and JJ without Hugh's guitar. Stabbing guitar ends it."

"'Peasant In The Big Shitty' – great live and also on the free single. This is a studio version. Dave is the voice but Jet opens with some skins. He sets the main beat and then the band closes in. Really good, has a different flavour to the live version. Hugh casually chants 'You're not real, oh no you're not, just a peasant in the big shitty.' The end is really great. Dave's voice goes off in a tangent on the crest of a tape loop. The main riff gets suspended before it crashes down."

"'Burning Up Time' – This one is about the Finchley boys. Sung by JJ, real acid guitar from Hugh yet again. The riff gets more and more involved. It starts to repeat and underneath it all Hugh comes on 'Does your mummy know where you are? Do you want a sweety?' At least I think it is Hugh, if not it is JJ! 'English Towns' – another completely new one that refers to the last tour of the country."

"'School Mam' – as the last number ends you can hear the happy sound of children playing in a school playground. One of the band's greatest numbers is underway. JJ's bass slices through. The end of the number is like some Hendrix LPs where he just twangs and lets the echoes close it. The guitars fall back. Jet collapses, he has been standing up all throughout the set. Dave can't see himself in the mirror. JJ and Hugh have turned into pillars of salt. Playtime again."

Melody Maker reported in September that; "The Stranglers released their first album in April of this year. It has sold more than a quarter of a million copies so far. A second album, *No More Heroes*, comes out later this month. This time next month The Stranglers will probably have two albums in the chart. This time last year they were nothing. The Stranglers' rise has been swift and, to some, painful. They now stand as a reminder never to underestimate the underdog. To the music business they seemed singularly un-together, and to the new wave they just didn't look right. They have shot us all down. They are one of the few bands to have emerged from the new wave with a sound of their own. Hear a Stranglers record, and you know right away it is them. It's a combination of Hugh Cornwell's brash vocal and understated guitar lines, Jean-Jacques Burnel's throbbing and echoey bass attacks, Dave Greenfield's dominant keyboard action, and Jet Black's frantic drum machine. Altogether, it's magic."

The Stranglers 1977

Chapter Four

Touring

In 1976 when The Stranglers were playing to pubs, beer was cheap (by today's standards at least!) and it wasn't uncommon for landlords to be able to expect a full house every night. In that regard, for many bands playing the pub scene, a ready-made audience was on offer. Just as it had taken some time to win audiences over in London, a tour of the UK was a new challenge.

Jet Black told *Sideburns* at the beginning of the year; "It's growing now. All the London gigs seem to be going okay. There are a lot of people in London who know our music and like it, so it's really great in London, but the reaction we are getting out of town is gradually changing in the same way it changed in London. I mean the first London gigs that we did we were booed off stage — people didn't understand that we were trying to do something different... We have got all our press cuttings from the beginning, and it's interesting to read through them because in all the early reviews they say that we are awful and terrible, and that our music is uninteresting and boring, but as you read through them over the months you see the same writers changing their point of view, and today they are saying 'Oh, we have really got something — the music is great.' I don't know if that means we've changed all that much, I don't think we have. I accept that what we're doing is valid."

Their first visit to Scotland was highly anticipated. The *Aberdeen Evening Express* reported in February; "One group who have emerged in the new wave with reputedly something to offer are The Stranglers, who begin their first tour outside London in Aberdeen on Friday night. The Stranglers have had their share of trouble like the others. After a gig at the Rainbow last week, the Greater London Council are reported as saying that they were taking a stand against The Stranglers. The row brewed after the band's guitarist and singer Hugh Cornwell appeared on stage with a t-shirt which had a f-f-four letter word on it. The show was stopped early and allegations were made after that a punk rock blacklist was being operated."

Cornwell's comedic banter with the audience comes across on the bootleg of the gig that took place at Glasgow's Queen Margaret University where he tells them that he doesn't understand their dialect. Despite the poor sound quality, on a bootleg of the gig that took place in Falkirk at the Miniqui Hall on 13th February, it is evident that The Stranglers are a tight sounding band in full control of their material. Later that month, a bootleg from the gig that took place in Middlesbrough at The Rock Gardens on 24th February includes Cornwell having a go at the audience for not dancing! The Stranglers played at Hawick Town Hall on 7th March. The gig concluded with a fight involving the venue's bouncers.

Such was the flexibility of the dates and venues as the tour moved along that apparently, gigs in Paris, Helsinki and Geneva had been pencilled in for late April. They didn't go ahead though. Burnel was quoted in *Strangled* from an interview that took place in May; "Paris is an interesting scene as far as I'm concerned. I really wanted to play there because it means a lot to me. The French have just discovered rock and roll in recent years. They are in the process of developing their own rock and roll culture, as opposed to pinching it from England and America. As yet it is a young culture and some of the familiar trappings are there. There is quite a strong punk/new wave scene, unfortunately Parisians have always been very image conscious and that's their big hang-up... I like the fact that a lot of the bands are singing in French, there is no need to sing in English. They have their own roots. Rock and roll is folk music and it should reflect what's going on around them. If you sing in English you don't communicate on a folk level, and *folk is the people.*"

A gig at the Roundhouse was reviewed in *Sounds* in April; "It's difficult to know where to start. I mean, I could tell you about the queue of people almost one hundred yards long that had to be turned away because the Roundhouse was full up. And I could waste a line or two on The Jam. Paul Weller and Bruce Foxton in their black suits, right legs pumping Beatles-style, Rickenbacker guitars slung round their necks, and Rick Buckler at the drums turning on high-energy — who that justly earned The Jam the kind of encore the Roundhouse rarely affords the band at the bottom. Or else I could try a thumbnail sketch of Cherry Vanilla (getting a little fat my dear) but with her wild red hair, black stockings, and gold lame hotpants, walking on the wild side of high camp cabaret."

"But it was The Stranglers who topped the bill. I've seen them play good gigs and I've seen diabolical ones, but I've never seen them approach the heights they scaled at the Roundhouse on their first headlining appearance in a major London venue. They rise to the occasion with the best set I've ever seen them play. How many promising young bands have you seen burn themselves out once they gain mass acceptance? Too many, right? Not so The Stranglers."

"Of course, they aired many of the tracks from their debut album, *Rattus Norvegicus* — how could they gig without 'Peaches', 'Grip', 'Down In The Sewer' or 'Sometimes'? But it was new ones like 'Whatever Happened To The Hero' (sic) and the amazing 'I Feel Like A Wog' (realism not racism) that will decide their future. Confident to the point of arrogance, The Stranglers dominated a packed house of screaming, gesticulating and pogoing kids. Loud and clear, they mixed that intense new wave beat with moments of pure psychedelia that would put Pink Floyd or Hawkwind to shame."

"Hugh Cornwell and Jean-Jacques Burnel hunted down the audience like urban guerrillas, while behind them Dave Greenfield washed the stage with a steady torrent of bubbling and boiling organ chords that added colour to Jet Black's heart attack drumming. If The Stranglers play many more gigs like this, they will be huge before the summer's out, mark my words."

On a bootleg of a Roundhouse performance (it could either be from the 16th or the 17th of April — it's not labelled clearly), 'No More Heroes' is introduced as a new song. An interesting choice considering that the *Rattus Norvegicus* album would be released just days after this gig. The Stranglers also refer to the suicide of Dagenham Dave.

In April 1977, *Record Mirror* reviewed the Roundhouse gigs; "Torrid scenes at London's Roundhouse when The Stranglers hit town this week. The fact that a large number of people were turned away is a measure of the meteoric rise to fame of the band once referred to as "Patti Smith's support group". They played most of their new album (which incidentally has advance orders of 15,000) and threw in one or two fresh numbers like 'I Feel Like A Wog' and 'Whatever Happened To The Hero' (sic). No more a band to watch. Just avoid the dust as they go stampeding on."

The same month they did a session for Capital Radio but it wasn't broadcast. They played 'Hanging Around', 'Goodbye Toulouse', 'I Feel Like A Wog', 'No More Heroes' and 'Dagenham Dave'.

The reason for the session not having been broadcast seems to remain unknown but it is unlikely that there was any bad blood between the band and the radio station. Regarding getting minimal airplay on Radio One, Black told *Record Mirror* in August 1977; "I rarely listen to Radio One, I listen to Capital most of the time, they play our music. But I think Alan Freeman and Anne Nightingale as well as John Peel play them."

Regarding how the tour was going, Burnel was quoted in *Strangled* from an interview that took place in May 1977; "It's going very well... We wouldn't be doing it if we didn't enjoy it. I don't consider it as work, although it's sometimes pretty tiring. To me, *work* is an evil. The term work is a four letter word and it's an evil that some people do to survive. I don't see why any person should... That's the difference between a slave and an artisan."

The gig that took place in Brunel University in the Kingdom Room on 20th May was reviewed in the student newspaper; "What can you say about The Stranglers? Nothing if you saw them! But if you were complacent enough not to, here's what you missed. Misgivings about punk rock because you associate the obnoxious/energetic petulance with serious political possibilities will remain simply healthy scepticism but if you're just disgusted by the way punks dress and carry on you may be just old and justicated. Gaba gaba!"

"Their first recording prospect came with Arista Records about a year ago when there was no punk scene to speak of, apart from The Stranglers and the Pistols that is! That flopped and it was only much later that Andrew Lauder of United Artists made the "common rat" possible. The music's main influence is definitely in The Doors and this is easily recognisable and readily admitted by the group's bassist Jean-Jacques Burnel ('I reckon that they were about the only band I ever listened to, there wasn't much else. Apart from The Nightingales and the Windsor Hell's Angels.')."

"So The Stranglers are mean ('some day I'm gonna smack your face')? Not really but the people of 'Toulouse' in France are. They liked the band so much down there that they've banned them. So The Stranglers dedicated Toulouse a song. Peach! 'London Lady' is about boring dolls and inflatable pollution ('plastic's real when you're real sick.'). And they've got a social conscience as developed as Lord Lichfield's, it's true only the fucking wealthy can be good looking! No really, The Stranglers are a new wave band and as such combine a new style and energy with their own observations of the sewer we all have to live in. Their energy is exciting and their attitude is for you to judge. It you are not angry about anything that goes on around you then you won't like The Stranglers."

There was no encore at this performance but they had their reasons. Burnel told *Sounds* in June; "People said we didn't do an encore 'cos we've got too big, but in fact, Hugh Cornwell was suffering from a bad attack of flu and he actually collapsed in the dressing room when we came off stage."

If the reviewer's observation was an accurate one, it's interesting to consider that within the band, some of the members were keener on the references to The Doors than others. It was asserted in *Zigzag* in June; "Phil McNeill's very interesting review of the album in NME, where he noted the misogynistic qualities of the songs, must be echoed. The negative vibes which permeate this record are very oppressive when careful attention is paid. But you don't have to listen that carefully to realise that this is a very good first LP indeed. The main musical influence seems to be The Doors, no doubt because Greenfield grew up with their first three albums, but The Stranglers aren't as clean. Their vocal harmonies on the other hand are exemplary, and I have to confess to looking forward to their next album. And what's all this crap about rats?"

Although the reviewer suggested that Greenfield had been influence by The Doors, it is apparently the case that the former had barely even listened to the latter! In actual fact, it wasn't until The Stranglers' early rehearsals that Cornwell had noticed the likeness between the two. On balance though, as Cornwell explained to *Melody Maker* in May; "I don't rush back after a gig and put on *Strange Days* for some new ideas to rip off. We do have the same line-up as The Doors but Dave had never heard of them until he met us. He was more into Yes and stuff like that." Black told *Record Mirror* in August; "I don't follow anyone's style deliberately. I mean I don't go out, watch a band and the detailed methods of the drummer. I was taught the basics and have taken it from there."

The bootleg of the gig that took place at Manchester's Electric Circus on 5th June is an interesting one. Not only were The Stranglers playing with high energy to a welcoming audience, but there are some fascinating nuggets of audience interaction included too; with Manchester being Dagenham Dave's hometown, he gets a mention and after 'Grip' being played as the opening number, a loud "fucking hell" is unapologetically said by one of the band.

The gig set for 9th June at Torquay Town Hall was

cancelled. Uncomfortably perhaps, although the council stipulated that they weren't willing to take the risk of having The Stranglers play at the venue, they refused to clarify what it was that they actually considered the risk to be. As a result, several farcical rumours came to the fore, including one that the council's main concern was that they didn't want young people to be at risk of being exposed to swearing.

Burnel said; "It seems to be that we may be unacceptable to some because our hair isn't parted in the right place or because we don't buy our clothes in certain shops and we don't go about with a lot of other ponces, poncing about. That's why the Finchley boys respect us and dig us. They are real people. Some of them work for a living and they don't go around making a big deal about dole queues because to them that is the worst thing that could happen to them. They don't like it and they don't capitalise on it, they are hard working kids and although we don't claim to be working class spokesmen, they relate to us because we try to be as straight as possible with them... They have been with us for about a year and they have developed into a hardcore elite. They know who they are and won't take any crap."

Sounds reported in July; "To paraphrase Jonathan Richman, I still love the sixties, and I still love the old world. Despite my interest in the new wave, The Doors are still my favourite band and *Forever Changes* is still my favourite LP. That's why I was initially attracted to The Stranglers. Yes, kids, the spirit of good ol' psychedelia lives on in their music. Their gig at Doncaster's house of flickers, the Gaumont, was a goodie. They played such numbers as 'Ugly', 'Go Buddy Go', which I can never hear without being reminded of 'Little Old Lady From Pasadena' (Go Granny Go), 'School Mam', 'Peaches' — a bad song, period, and 'I

Feel Like A Wog'. The latter selection is interesting — for days after I first heard it I was haunted by it."

"Lyrically, The Stranglers haven't distinguished themselves yet but on 'Wog', a vignette about paranoia, they actually use inarticulacy to very good effect. Good music too, when they are at their best ('Down In The Sewer', 'Peasant In The Big Shitty', dopey lyrics notwithstanding, 'School Mam' etc.), They can't be beaten — the throbbing rhythm section, the spectral guitar, the calliope-like organ flourishes straight out of *Something Wicked This Way Comes*."

"Just blur your eyes and let the music transport you. You're watching The Doors at the Whisky, the Velvets at the Dom. The Stranglers don't look like a chart-topping band though. They are really as gristly and unappetising as specimens from a *Reader's Wives* page. Burnel does his best to come on sullen and mean, in which consists the whole art and duty of punkhood, but doesn't convince. And his singing — the word is a euphemism — isn't too good either. Cornwell looks like he arrived at the theatre on an old pushbike. Jet and Dave, frankly, look too old and pudgy to be playing a set of identikit "anarchists" fresh out of secondary school. But they are a fine, fine band. To hell with it."

"Oh, halfway through 'Go Buddy Go' Jean-Jacques and Hugh leapt into the audience and conducted a little business. That was interesting. But the best part of the set, during a second reading of the same song, was when all the kids down front went apeshit and clambered up onstage to dance around and play their imaginary guitars and so on. A beautiful celebration of youthful energy — touching, even."

The gig that took place at Eric's in Liverpool was originally supposed to happen elsewhere in the city. It was reported in the *Liverpool Echo* on 16th June 1977; "Punk rock group The Stranglers will not be appearing at Liverpool's Empire Theatre next Sunday — but just who made that decision is in some dispute. The Empire's manager, Mr Charles O'Neill, said that he had made the decision to cancel the show — 'they're not suitable attractions for the Empire.' But, The Stranglers' manager Mr Derek Savage, said the group had cancelled because they could not reach an agreement about covering over the orchestra pit at the theatre — 'they don't like playing that far away from the audience — there's not enough contact,' he said."

"Mr O'Neill said that ticket sales had been going well but he had cancelled because 'I don't want to see young people being influenced in a way that could be prevented. They appear on the stage with a contraceptive in one ear and a safety pin in the other. I don't think that the theatre — and certainly the Empire — is the place for this.' The decision to cancel has been made after adverse reports had been received, but the group will be appearing in the city on Eric's in Matthew Street."

How surreal that people were arguing to take the credit as to why the gig at the Empire was cancelled! I would have thought it would have made more sense if The Empire were keen to deny their part in being killjoys! Unless of course, from Savage's point of view, it was empowering to denounce the Empire's suitability for a Stranglers gig.

When asked where he preferred in England outside of London, Burnel told *Shews*; "Liverpool. It's just a great place. They are very intelligent people, they're very spontaneous. They have treated us with respect. They understand us. There's a gig in Liverpool called Eric's. It used to be called The Cavern. It's all decorated in "art-deco" style. They've also got papier-mashe heads of The Beatles. We were wondering whether to burn them, or not.

We drew little moustaches on them. But we decided that they were valid 'cos they were a tribute to a dead era."

And in *Strangled*; "There are a lot of good people in Liverpool... It's a very good scene. There is a very positive feeling in Liverpool — they want to elevate themselves."

It was reported in *North Wales Weekly News* in June; "The Stranglers' date in Bangor in October is one of three concerts already lined up by the university students in the autumn, and more seem likely to follow. The gig will form part of a big British tour by the group to promote the follow-up album to *Rattus Norvegicus*, presently in the top ten LP charts. But the price of fame to local rock fans means they will have to fork out £2.20 for a ticket. When The Stranglers played to a students-only concert in Bangor just six months ago, the fee was £90. This time it's over £1,000, which is one of the biggest sums paid out to a band by the students' entertainments committee."

"Nevertheless, promoter Kevin Elliott is confident that there will be a full house. With tickets for the whole tour being sold through agencies, he predicts a heavy demand from a wide area, and advises those who want to go to get their tickets well in advance to avoid disappointment. The phenomenal rise of The Stranglers has allowed them to veer away steadily from the "punk" tag. It's obviously something which has helped them to achieve their present status, but it is also something that is putting their present tour into a state of chaos. The merest mention of the word "punk" has sent councils rushing to ban the group from various civic halls. The next album has already been recorded — at the same time the first LP was conceived — but it is still possible that some tracks may be re-recorded in the light of experience."

"There will also be a follow-up to the controversially worded single 'Peaches' in August. The next offering will be worth waiting for, because *Rattus Norvegicus* is a gritty, vibrant LP, displaying quite a few influences and straight "nicks" from sixties bands, yet unleashing it from a freshly-tapped source of power. The record is musically streets ahead of some of the "new wave" contemporaries. Listen to their single, '(Get A) Grip (On Yourself)' or to such tracks from the LP as 'Goodbye Toulouse' or 'Hanging Around' for an insight into the band's music."

This article pretty much hits the nail on the head in terms of how the punk label was probably something of a double-edged sword for the band; on the one hand it had promotional power on the basis of notoriety but on the other, it sometimes resulted in the band being tarred with a brush that simply didn't apply to them and their music.

Besides, it is possible that The Stranglers were a band of the people. It was advocated in *New Musical Express* in October; "The Stranglers are a band who do their best to keep prices down, who are against record business receptions and related liggerama, who want to be with *real people*, and who are going to be the most idolised heroes in rock/pop culture."

A fair assessment considering that in August, *North Wales Weekly News* reported: "Ticket prices for the proposed gig by The Stranglers at Bangor in October have been brought down — by order of the group. The band asked their management agency to renegotiate the deal with the city's students when they heard that tickets would cost £2.20. So the price has now been dropped to £1.75. The Stranglers will be naming their own support band and will be providing a disco for the concert on 8th October. The gig is part of a thirty-date British tour to promote their second album, *No More Heroes*."

"The LP, due out on 16th September, will feature their present single, 'Something Better Change'. Plans for the concert are going ahead despite protests from the local community council, who want to have the group banned. The latest position is that the students have asked for a meeting with councillors to allay their fears, but the community council have decided to wait and see what support comes for their attempt at a ban. Tickets have been printed, and a few are now available by personal application to the Student's Union. But most of the tickets will not go on sale until the week of the concert when students return. As the concert is a "freshers' week" event, the organisers felt that it might jeopardise their chances of getting tickets if they went on sale beforehand."

"With The Stranglers' debut album, *Rattus Norvegicus*, still in the British top ten, it is highly likely that the concert could be sold out even without the support of students. The group's last big tour in May was hit by several enforced cancellations, but their recent appearances on *Top Of The Pops* — often the acid-test of acceptance by middle-aged councillors — look to have cooled matters down."

It seems a shame to consider that an appearance on *Top Of The Pops* may have been regarded as the point at which a band could be considered "acceptable" in the mainstream as in, did it really take such "seal of approval" for a band to get the thumbs up from a wider proportion of society?! Damn! That's harsh! With it being pre-internet days with only three TV channels though, maybe an appearance on *Top Of The Pops* was, rightly or wrongly, something of a necessary evil for some bands.

Burnel said; "We wanted to be on *Top Of The Pops* because it is a folk medium — the most accessible medium, and we wanted to communicate. Nevertheless, we are involved in inverted snobbery. *Top Of The Pops* is a lightweight programme, and it's become lightweight because I think that in recent years certain rock bands thought that the singles market was too lightweight and so they didn't contribute to make it a broader scene. There is no reason why we shouldn't return to the excitement of the sixties in that respect, that raw live scene – when the single was supreme. That's what is good about a lot of the new bands, they are all writing potential singles so they might as well use the singles medium to expose themselves but you've got a problem now – we are meant to be miming, but no way are we that kind of band."

Later in the interview it was revealed that Burnel and Cornwell swapped guitars for their *Top Of The Pops* performance as a nod towards the fact that they weren't too pleased about having to mime.

It's a good thing that the dates in Wales were able to go ahead really. It was reported in *North Wales Weekly News* in July; "Why they want to throttle those "harmless" Stranglers – The backlash against punk rock and anything remotely connected with it has now landed on the doorstep of concert-goers in North Wales. The latest reaction has come from a committee of Bangor councillors who want to throttle proposals by students in the city to stage a show by The Stranglers in October. The move has once again thrown up the thorny question of local censorship. Councillors uttered phrases last week such as 'rubbish', 'immoral' and 'diabolical' without, presumably, ever having listened to The Stranglers, and it is unlikely that they will take up the offer of the group's publicity officer who has said he will send the council a copy of the LP, *Rattus Norvegicus*, if they give him a ring."

"For the group, the local controversy is just adding to the wave of reaction against them by councils all over the country during their present trouble-torn British tour. The Stranglers had to cancel a couple of gigs recently following a reported fracas with police after a show in Cleethorpes.

Their drummer, Jet Black, hurt a hand during the incident. But however fast some councils are moving to ban them, there is a queue of promoters waiting in line to book them for alternative dates. The Stranglers are big business, and more than thirty dates — including the one at Bangor — have been confirmed for the forthcoming autumn tour. At least one Bangor councillor had the sense to see that making a big issue of the matter was just giving more publicity to the group."

"Their debut LP has been in the top ten for several weeks. Perhaps if local rock fans were given the chance of seeing The Stranglers, they could decide for themselves whether the group is 'inoffensive', as their publicity officer describes them, or 'rubbish', 'diabolical' and 'immoral' as some councillors view them. I would suspect that the truth lies in between."

Regarding the aforementioned Black fracas on 2nd July *Record Mirror* reported that Jet had been "involved in an incident with the local constabulary" after a gig in Cleethorpes and that he had injured his hand in the fracas to the extent that he was unable to play the following two gigs booked for Bristol and Bracknell, despite having managed to play the dates at the London Roundhouse post-injury.

It was claimed in the report that £2,000 worth of earnings had been lost as a result of the cancelled gigs (that wasn't the only hand injury sustained in the year — when The Stranglers posed for a photo in Manchester prior to their gig at the Electric Circus on 5th June, it is clear that Burnel's hand is heavily bandaged, apparently from an injury sustained at the Wigan Casino the previous night).

It's fascinating to consider just how many stakeholders were affected by a Stranglers tour date, even when one was cancelled due to illness. It was reported in the

Reading Evening Post on 27th June; "Disappointed punk rock fans were turned away from Bracknell Sports Centre on Saturday night after a concert by the controversial band The Stranglers was suddenly cancelled. Many were later barred from entering pubs in the town because, one landlord said today, they looked underage. The concert, which councillors had demanded to be called off, was eventually cancelled because Jet Black suddenly fell ill. But it should still go ahead within the next few weeks if the promoter and the sports centre management can fix a new date."

"It appeared that word got around that the concert had been cancelled, and only a few dozen fans turned up at the sports centre. There was no trouble when they were told the concert was off. Most went home but some tried to get into pubs in the area. The Horse and Groom pub, just a few hundred yards from the sports centre in Bagshot Road, opened one and a quarter hours late, at 7:15pm. Landlord, Mr Trevor Whalley, then stood at the door and turned a number of punk rock fans away. He said today, 'The ones who were turned away were all under eighteen. I have got nothing against punk rockers, but I thought that all the people I refused entry to were underage'."

"Several fans were also turned away from the Market Inn, opposite Bracknell Station, for the same reason. Sports centre manager Mr Joe Farrell said today, 'The drummer was taken ill and the doctor he went to said he couldn't perform. There is a possibility of rearranging the concert, but no firm date has been set for it. Not many people actually turned up. A lot of people phoned up during the afternoon to ask if it was true whether it had been cancelled.' Mr Farrell came under attack from some councillors for booking the band."

"The group have been banned from venues up and

down the country after outbreaks of violence and damage to public halls at concerts on their British tour. One councillor claimed it was 'irresponsible' of Mr Farrell to book The Stranglers. The band has had both an album and a single in the pop charts and was expected to draw a big crowd to the 2,000 capacity sports centre. The town's police feared there would be outbreaks of drunken violence at the concert. Last week, Bracknell magistrates agreed to a police application for the sports centre's bar opening hours to be cut back for Saturday night."

"The concert was being organised by promoter Mr Allan Smith, of Burlesque Enterprises, who usually promotes concerts at the sports centre. Police had decided not to put men on duty at the concert after they were assured by Mr Smith that he would take all necessary security measures. He had hired a number of security men to keep order during the concert. The district council's chief recreation officer said he was satisfied all adequate precautions had been taken and that there would have been no trouble at the concert."

On 2nd July *Melody Maker* reported; "An amusing scene at the climax of The Stranglers' first house recital last Sunday at London's Roundhouse. The audience grooved to the mundane rhythms of this ever-popular combo, one pretty lady was so overcome with passionate excitement that she rushed through the jiving throng, clambered onstage and made a kamikaze rush towards Hugh Cornwell, the group's immensely talented guitarist and vocalist. Her ambition, no doubt, was merely to express her gratitude and thanks to the immensely talented Cornwell for articulating so precisely through his music the aspirations and desires of his fans. Alas, her way towards her hero was barred by two "stewards", who instantly bundled her offstage in a less than polite and ceremonious fashion (i.e.

she was dragged into the wings)."

Cornwell, justifiably incensed by this incident, swung his guitar through the air and smashed it violently onto the stage, the crunch and spattering fretboard and ensuing feedback echoed noisily through the hall. The report suggesting that it was considered by some to be the nearest The Stranglers have yet come to producing any noteworthy music!

Cornwell rushed after the trio, fists clenched and teeth bared. The confrontation that followed was, unfortunately, hidden by the discreet positioning of a speaker.

Undaunted by the fate of her companion, another young lady boarded the stage and unopposed, enjoyed a lengthy embrace with J.J. Deliriously happy, she eventually came up for air and returned quietly to the audience. It proved that the too-often rough-house tactics by bouncers wasn't always called for.

Record Mirror reported in July; "I'm fed up with reviewing Stranglers concerts. Screwing words to fit white spaces. Saturation level reached. Nothing more to say. Nice to go along and simply see them without making any hollow analysis. Right, I've got fifteen minutes to write this — two shows at the Roundhouse. Queues along the Chalk Farm Road. Staple guns in Camden. Around 6,000 tickets sold in one week. Reporters from the Guinness book of hot shots abounded. First show — sober. This fair land's strange licensing hours prevented a lot of people having a better time. The band (I thought Hugh Cornwell was dead anyway) played. Played very well in fact. Probably never played better. Lots of healthy new songs too. Second show — Bar room blitz. Audience reaction one over the eight. Dedicated followers of fashion loving every minute. The band played again. Played very well again. Er, then they finished. Peachy. End of a tour. And what a bummer summer. This is getting ridiculous."

A lovely roundabout way of saying that, as the reviewer had experienced plenty of times before, The Stranglers were good. Notably, the review was written by Barry Cain who also travelled to The Paradiso in Amsterdam to interview The Stranglers later in the year when they were casually hanging out with the Hell's Angels. Cain probably had a good idea of what to expect from a Stranglers gig having met them a few times throughout 1977.

A bootleg of the gig in Stockholm in August 1977 didn't come with the best sound quality but it is noteworthy because it documents what are possibly early live performances of '5 Minutes', 'Dead Ringer' and 'Bring On The Nubiles'. By this point in the year, 'Peaches' was not only a well-known track in the UK but, according to this bootleg at least, it was met with enthusiasm by the crowd in Sweden too.

From the point of view of the venues, a lot of thought was still going into whether or not to let The Stranglers play. In September *Reading Evening Post* reported; "Stranglers punk band to visit Reading — Controversial star punk rock band The Stranglers have been booked to appear at Reading's Top Rank Suite at the end of next month. News of the band's date at the town comes while there is still strong opposition to a proposed appearance at Bracknell Sports Centre this month, because of fears of violence and disorder from their audience. The band will be playing on October 30th, said a spokesman for Rank Leisure Services in London. The organisation has decided to take no extra precautions when they appear. Mr Harry Johnson, of Rank Leisure Services said 'We regard it as just another concert and the band as just a new wave group. We do not feel there is any need to take any special precautions. As far as we are concerned it is a normal straightforward tour.' He added the band was booked to appear at other Top Rank suites in the country."

"A bid to ban the band from their Bracknell appearance was narrowly defeated in July. But the group — labelled 'repulsive' by some councillors — will only be allowed to play at the Centre if they guarantee to cover any loss of income caused by any damage done. Bracknell councillors claimed the group's performance, scheduled for September 24th, could lead to a violent rampage by teenagers. A previous concert by the group, cancelled at the last minute through illness, brought dozens of punk rockers to Bracknell. The band's impending arrival in Reading has brought no worries to local councillors. Deputy Tory leader Simon Coombs said he did not think their audiences were particularly violent. 'A few years ago people might have said the same thing about a rock festival in Reading,' he said. The concert was to be on private property and — unless the peace was disrupted — not the council's concern. Labour leader Bob Garnett said what went on in the Top Rank Suite was a matter for the Rank organisation. Liberal group leader Jim Day said he could not comment on the booking as he had no knowledge of the group."

I love how the reporter endeavoured to find out what each representative of the three main political parties made of the matter. I'm bursting to comment on the idiosyncrasies that spring to mind, but in the interests of maintaining a balanced narrative, I'll leave it there.

District councillor Bill Brown had voted to ban The Stranglers from playing at the sports centre. He told the *Reading Evening Post*; "We heard the usual case about freedom and that they will finish themselves off through lack of support but if one looks around the community now after several years of this attitude, the sight isn't a pretty one, with rising crime and VD on the increase."

Apparently music causes crime and VD! Who'd have thunk it! Nuts to all the naysayers really, especially considering that in *New Musical Express* in October 1977, the journalist described how The Stranglers were welcomed when they performed at Bracknel Sports Centre; "The second date of the tour gets a reception of mass orgasm so rapturous that it would appear The Stranglers are now achieving such mass worship proliferation that their policy of playing only venues with no seats will be virtually impossible. It's like a sauna in the gig with numerous pogoers flaking out."

Regarding the councils who cancelled gigs, Burnel told *Sounds* in June; "The best form of censorship is individual. It's an over-reaction on the part of the councils and shows how insecure they are."

An agreeable point really; nobody can control everything that's around them but personally and intellectually, there is a lot to be said for respecting the individual to make their own choices about what they do or don't expose themselves to. Nobody *has to* watch a horror film. Nobody *has to* go on a rollercoaster. If you don't like something, boycott it and leave others to enjoy it. When it came to The Stranglers and many of the stigmas surrounding their image in 1977, this was probably going to be the most sensible approach, particularly on the sexism front. As with many things in life, it probably comes down to what an individual makes of it.

On the 1st August, The Stranglers played at the Rotterdam Festival. When one of the crowd got too close to the stage, Cornwell chastised him by telling him to go and "wank in the toilets".

The bootleg of the 2nd September gig at Amsterdam's Paradiso is a fascinating one because, if the reports of what The Stranglers' time was like in Amsterdam later that year is anything to go by, perhaps they were more than a little bit distracted there. It's not my place to say either way but on the bootleg, Cornwell doesn't deliver some of the lyrics on 'No More Heroes' and when playing 'London Lady', the band stop altogether in order to play it again from the top. Despite this, the crowd chants for more. A fantastic document of The Stranglers being welcomed by a receptive audience just days prior to the release of *No More Heroes* on 16th September.

The gig that took place at Cambridge Corn Exchange was the opening night of the *No More Heroes* tour. It was reviewed in *New Musical Express* in October 1977; "Whatever happened to — the existentialist heroes, or the di Niroes? It's true — for most people there *are* no more heroes — only group therapy. Safety in numbers — dress by numbers, dance by numbers... My all too western mind was plagued with preconception over The Stranglers — yes, that's right, the sexist bit. Well, almost, because my objections were never motivated by any crusading spirit for the, er, sisters — just that I've always found any manifestations of the macho-see macho-do projection in pop kulture (sic) to be somewhat infantile."

"Having said that — blow over sainthood — they came over about as sexist as the National Front are humanist. In fact, they came over as nothing if not bored, little or no effort made to win over the crowd with sexist remarks or otherwise an atmosphere less-than-zero. As the set wore on I began to realise that the Only Ones (the support band) weren't the only ones, anachronism wise. I mean these guys are strange heroes — no short back and spikes, no contempo "This City Will Be The Death Of Me" imagery, and Greenfield playing with increasing weirdness on the ivorys — psychedelia rampant for a change of gear (velocity) and a dance that doesn't hammer the law of gravity with such force."

"As for the music, I found it all a bit sick and detached. They may be more accomplished instrumentally than the majority of the new wave, but they don't seem to play with any conviction, live force. Certainly not enough light and shade. They played 'Straighten Out', 'Bring On The Nubiles', 'Sometimes', 'Dagenham Dave', 'Dead Ringer' (everyone greeting it, apparently as 'Peaches', which they didn't play), 'Hanging Around', 'Peasant In The Big Shitty', 'I Feel Like A Wog', a new song called '5 Minutes', 'London Lady', 'No More Heroes' and 'Something Better Change'."

"Somewhere into 'Grip', the first number of the "encore", two "chicks" materialised on stage and proceeded to do what can best be described as a mindless, formless, moron cheerleader dance, going on to clutch Cornwell and Burnel in a manner that would have made Woody and Les envious. No attempt was made to get rid of them, even by heavies or The Stranglers themselves – who looked as if they were past caring. More and more people followed suit on the stage until the band – by now ploughing through an unscheduled(?) instrumental(?) – was totally obscured by the frenzied mob."

What a strange review! It may as well have said something like "group with reputation for being sexist doesn't actually do anything sexist". Also, the fact that some of the crowd joined The Stranglers onstage could have been portrayed as something endearing and positive rather than something that occurred as a result of lazy crowd control. It sounds like the reviewer wasn't as excited to be at the gig as some of the fans were!

On the bootleg of the Canterbury Odeon gig that took place on 25th September, the renditions of 'Something Better Change' and 'Bitching' absolutely sparkle (not only due to the good sound quality of this particular bootleg but the performance of the songs in and of themselves).

They introduce '5 Minutes' (so much so that Burnel's vocals seem to wonder off a bit) as a new number. Cornwell's rapport with the audience comes across as something of a mixed bag; he goes from telling them that they don't need seats to asking them to refrain from spitting.

In October, *Sounds* reviewed a gig that took place in Uxbridge; "Of course, what with all those bad reviews The Stranglers have picked up since the release of the new album *No More Heroes*, you might expect the band's popularity to be on the wane. But don't let those greying hacks and esoteric schizophrenics fool you. They didn't fool the students at Brunel and the punks from Harrow."

"An hour after the doors were open, as support band Wire were about to begin, the crowd lines outside would have to be measured to be believed. Whenever The Stranglers play Brunel it turns out to be a night worth remembering — and this one was certainly no different. I couldn't care what anybody else says, The Stranglers are still one of the finest rock 'n' roll bands this country has spawned in years. Old wave, new wave, fart, new fart, what do the labels matter, eh? Electric music is electric music. It either hits you where it should or else it apologises and passes by on the other side."

"And since when did The Stranglers ever apologise for anything? Not at Brunel, brother. They *were* patchy, even founder fan club members here will admit that. But only really in the sound. Jean-Jacques Burnel, suffering from *la rings dans* the throat, was singing a little off-key at times, but even so in just about every instance the vocals came over with a dynamic clarity many well-established rock bands find difficult to achieve. That meant no member of the audience had trouble recognising 'Ugly', 'Straighten Out', 'Bring On The Nubiles', 'Sometimes', 'Dagenham

Dave', 'Dead Ringer', 'Hanging Around', 'Bitching, 'I Feel Like A Wog', '5 Minutes' (a new number that feels like it's really going to stick), 'London Lady', 'No More Heroes', 'Something Better Change', and the encores 'Down In The Sewer' (complete with Burnel and Cornwell's rat waltz) and 'Go Buddy Go'."

"And no member of the audience can have felt divorced from the action either. Hugh Cornwell openly invited the kids up on stage next to him and so many accepted that the set ground to a halt twice and the stage had to be cleared before The Stranglers could draw breath and continue. But no one seemed to mind. It was just like one gigantic party with everybody having a good time and no windows smashed. And isn't that what rock 'n' roll is really all about?"

On 5th October, the *Coventry Evening Telegraph* review of the previous night's gig stated; "A better class of punk rockers — Tiffany's was last night in the firm grip of The Stranglers, who powered through a full throttle set. The place was thick and steamy like a sauna, as the squashed crowd swayed like spectators on Liverpool's Kop. On disc, The Stranglers are notable among the new wave in that they have produced some tolerable songs. But when they appeared at this Coventry venue in June, their live sound was appalling. They put that right last night — and they must now be running the danger of becoming middle-class punks, because their light show and choreography added an extra polish to the performance."

"Having said that, it would be easy to get carried away. Although they played for about an hour — and all the instruments could be heard — their compositions and capabilities still remain suspect. Basically they only have two songs. There's the slow 'Peaches' and the fast 'Something Better Change'. Everything else is a minute —

sometimes indistinguishable — variation of them. They do have an advantage of keyboards but all Dave Greenfield does with them is to repeat a simple riff beyond the point when it became memorable to the stage when it is monotonous. The Stranglers have been compared to The Doors — even if it only aspires to the squeak of the hinges."

That last comment from the reviewer was pretty damn biting! Where he states that the majority of the songs were indistinguishable, it raises the question as to whether they were being played differently to how they appear on record. The songs on both *Rattus Norvegicus* and *No More Heroes* are abundant in melodic hooks and ideas that make each of them very different to the others.

The Coventry gig was made possible because a ban had been lifted. It was reported in the *Coventry Evening Telegraph* in August; "Tiffany's in Coventry have lifted their ban on punk rock groups. During the next few months, some of the top punk groups in the country — including The Damned, The Clash, The Jam and The Stranglers — will be appearing. In June, The Clash were banned from giving a concert at Tiffany's following a riot by their fans at London's Rainbow Theatre when damage put at £2,500 was caused. The group will appear as a top-of-the-bill attraction at a concert on 8th November."

"Why the change of heart by Mecca — who own Tiffany's — over the new wave bands? Mr Aubrey Marsden, manager of Tiffany's, said 'We have had difficulties with this kind of band in the past but now they have realised that they can't get bookings if they cause trouble.' He said that a performance by The Stranglers in June had been a success although eggs and a glass were thrown at the group. The series of punk rock dates had been arranged by an outside agency, Endale Association, and the new generation rock stars had not been booked by Mecca, said

Mr Marsden. 'This means I cannot stop them appearing,' said Marsden, who is not a follower of punk, 'the only think the company draws the line at are striptease dancers,' he added."

The *North Wales Weekly News* reported on 13th October; "No more heroes — The Stranglers prove it — The Stranglers' appearance in Bangor on Saturday was an occasion. It was destined to be one long before the group had played a note. Perhaps that was why the concert never quite lived up to expectations. It was a good gig but lacked the consistent electricity to make it a great gig. The mere fact that one of the biggest draws in Britain were playing in a rock-starved area brought in a weird assortment of ardent fans, weekend punks, sceptic students and scene-seekers. And if anything, they were too tame for the band's liking."

"There was little trouble, and the only awkward moment came when Hugh Cornwell asked the squashed front row to stop spitting at him (funny how your best ideas sometimes backfire on you). Cornwell also put a microphone stand into the skull of a fan who got too enthusiastic. The Stranglers' set was brash, at times brilliant, and was over as quickly as it started. They motored through thirteen songs, opening somewhat quietly by their standards with 'Straighten Out' — the B-side of 'Something Better Change' — which included some great phrased vocals on the chorus. But the wheels really began turning with the harsh vocals of Jean-Jacques Burnel on 'Ugly'."

"The Rats On The Road showed off all the strengths which have taken both their albums into the top ten — notably Dave Greenfield's keyboards work. It invites obvious comparison with The Doors, but The Stranglers are the only group to have capitalised on that distinctive sound and made it their own. The material in the set was plucked from *Rattus Norvegicus* and *No More Heroes* with 'Hanging Around', 'Sometimes', 'London Lady', and 'Something Better Change' the highlights of the night. 'No More Heroes' brought the set to a close, and they encored with 'Down In The Sewer' with Burnel and Cornwell flashing their guitars into the faces of the fans who by now were pressed like wild flowers against the stage."

"The Stranglers would have come back to do 'Grip', but the audience's enthusiasm subsided quickly. Support band The Drones from Manchester put in a lively set, but I'm wondering how long The Stranglers can go on sharing the bill with bands that like playing gigs like this. If their promoter is right, and the band become as big a draw in Britain as The Rolling Stones by the end of this year, it could well be bye-bye Bangor, hello football stadiums for them."

The bootleg from the gig at Liverpool University that took place on 14th October includes snippets from (what seems to be!) the soundcheck. Songs that were not at all common to the regular setlist are played during this; 'English Towns' as well as a small snippet of 'In The Shadows'. A nice easy going jam session is featured too.

As with on the bootleg of an earlier gig, Burnel once again sounds like he might have lost his place during '5 Minutes' but on balance, it might have been a particularly challenging audience with regards to the comments on the spitting they were doing. Overall, the band sound tight and exuberant.

It would be unrealistic to see The Stranglers as victims when it came to them not being welcome back at some venues. It was reported in the *Newcastle Journal* in October; "It may be a long time before Tyneside next sees The Stranglers — and not just because the band has a busy schedule until Easter next year. After their appearance at

Newcastle City Hall last week, the city authorities will not be putting out the welcome mat again very quickly. The City Hall management are still annoyed at the band's interference in crowd control measures at the gig. The Stranglers ordered the city hall stewards not to intervene and said that their own road crew would deal with any problems."

"They did, but only after scores of enthusiastic fans had invaded the stage for a mass pogo session. The result — some damage to seats and plenty of hard words afterwards. To complete an unhappy stay in Newcastle, the police drugs squad raided the band's hotel in the early morning, questioning members of the band and their roadies. This week a spokesperson for The Stranglers defended the band's policy. 'The band have noticed that official stewards don't often seem to understand that the fans are just having fun — they may look violent but they're not — whereas their own road crew tend not to overreact.' But, however good the intentions, it is incidents like last week's which gives The Stranglers a "trouble making" image — and that rebounds on their fans."

"Already two sell-out shows in Dublin on their current tour have been cancelled by fearful authorities there. And the band's spring tour was cut by a third because of local councils banning The Stranglers from their premises. If Newcastle City Council imposes a Stranglers ban — official or unofficial — it leaves few alternative venues in the North East, especially as the Mayfair's management are not over-enthusiastic about punk bands. After all, The Stranglers are too big to settle for college bops any more."

Such damage wasn't an isolated incident. The gig at the Guildford Civic Hall on 29th May saw £700 worth of damage done to the seating area. Disappointing news considering what Newcastle made of The Stranglers' gig there earlier in the year.

One reader who had his letter printed in the *Newcastle Evening Chronicle* on 23rd June made an interesting point; "Having attended a punk rock concert on Wednesday i.e. The Stranglers at the City Hall, I feel I must write to complain at your lack of coverage of the event. No doubt had a row or two of seats been smashed, you would have made this front page news, but as the concert passed without any incidents you ignore it. It seems to me that the press go out of their way to make the general public feel that all of the punk rock scene is disgusting. However, if the sight of 2,000 people having a great time without harming anyone is disgusting, then heaven help us."

In the fanzine, *Summer Salt*, the Glasgow Apollo gig on the 16th October was reviewed the same month; "The queue was massive. It crocodiled round three sides of the block and during the long wait the crowd started singing 'Pretty Vacant' and 'No More Posers'. It promised to be some gig. A party of councillors was attending to see if this kind of show was "suitable" as the concert was almost banned from taking place."

"As I entered the hall the support group was already playing. They were those staunch representatives of Scottish new wave The Rezillos. As I took my seat they sang 'I Can't Stand My Baby' and The Rolling Stones oldie 'I Wanna Be Your Man', both sides of their double B-side single on Sensible Records. Leaving the stage to a hearty applause the bassist said into the mic, 'Scotland will rise again.' Too right mate!"

"During the twenty minute interval the DJ got the pogoers warmed up by playing records from The Drones, The Clash and The Dictators. Eventually the stage darkened and on they walked — The Stranglers — to a deafening roar. They kicked off with their current single, 'No More

Heroes'. At the end, Hugh Cornwell decided to have a word with the aforementioned councillors. 'Where's Mister Aitkin and his chums?' he rasped. The crowd shouted with pleasure and a spotlight was put on the council box. Then Hugh said, 'Don't judge any group by what we do. We don't represent anyone else. We're The Stranglers, right.' From then on the atmosphere grew."

"They played all their best numbers — 'Ugly', 'London Lady' and a few others from their new album such as 'Dagenham Dave' and 'I Feel Like A Wog' with Dave Greenfield taking over lead vocals for 'Dead Ringer'. The group also did a song I hadn't heard before called '5 Minutes'. The show finished all too quickly. It was pure magic. Everyone was out of their seats dancing at the end, we were all shouting for more."

"After what seemed like years The Stranglers returned to the stage — again to a deafening roar. They played 'Peaches' and 'Grip' and left the stage for a second time amid whistles and cheers and voices calling for more. Again the group returned and Hugh Cornwell shouted 'Are there any rats here?' There was a positive response and he said 'Good 'cos this one's for you' and launched into 'Down In The Sewer' with Jean-Jacques Burnel pogoing onstage and Hugh creeping round the keyboards with his guitar, looking for rats, no doubt. It was a brilliant number to end on. 'Let's hear your best cheer for The Stranglers,' said the DJ and the group finally left the stage to thunderous applause and requests for 'Go Buddy Go'. An evening to remember."

The bootleg of the gig at Sheffield Top Rank on 19th October is essential listening. The Stranglers are on top form (even though it *still* sounds as if Burnel is getting to grips with the lyrics on '5 Minutes').

Cornwell practically screams the introduction to

'Straighten Out'. The band leave the stage after playing 'London Lady' and it leaves the audience chanting their name, upon which they return to the stage to play 'Peaches' and 'Grip' for an encore.

At Birmingham's Mayfair Suite on 20th October they were supported by Steel Pulse. As a reggae band, Steel Pulse were less familiar with the audience culture of spitting at bands on stage. Apparently, as they were barely into playing their first song, a huge glob of phlegm landed on the bassist's (Ron "Stepper" McQueen) hand. He stopped playing and the rest of the band followed suit. Amongst the silence, Burnel, having identified the culprit, jumped into the crowd and knocked him out.

The tour was tarnished with legal matters that got personal towards the end of the year. The *Newcastle Journal* reported on 28th October; "Top punk rockers face court — Two members of the top punk rock group, The Stranglers, have been arrested after a concert. They will appear at Brighton Court on 15th November charged with obstruction and being drunk, said police."

"Bassist Jean-Jacques Burnel and drummer Jet Black, were arrested at Brighton police station with three others on Wednesday. The Stranglers, whose latest LP, *No More Heroes*, is number two in the *Melody Maker* chart this week had just finished a show at Brighton Top Rank. A group spokesman said the two were detained overnight by police, and released on £75 bail. When The Stranglers were in Newcastle for a concert recently, backstage workers were arrested after a drug squad raid at the Centre Hotel."

All's well that ends well though. Well, kind of! It was reported in the *Newcastle Journal* on 17th November; "Stranglers cleared of drunk charge — Two members of punk rock group The Stranglers were cleared by magistrates at Brighton, Sussex, yesterday of being drunk and disorderly and violent behaviour in the town's police station. They are Jethro "Jet" Black (sic), the group's drummer of Send, Surrey, and Jean-Jacques Burnel, the bass guitarist of Wandsworth, London. Their assistant tour manager, Dennis Marks of East Finchley, London was found not guilty of obstructing police. The three, who pleaded not guilty, were arrested at the police station after the group gave a concert in Brighton."

"The prosecution alleged that Black banged on the counter and Burnel drank two glasses of wine from a bottle he carried. Both were said to have been drunk and to have shouted, waved their arms and refused repeated requests to leave. Black said that, after the concert, the group returned to their dressing room. He was staggered to see policemen with a dog emerge from a roof hatchway and search the room. Later, he heard two Hell's Angels had been arrested in the auditorium and he went to the police station to enquire about them. 'Hell's Angels are among our most ardent fans,' said Black, who claimed that a police sergeant at the station was uncooperative and wanted them to get out. Then he and Burnel were arrested. 'I could see no reason why I was treated in this way. I was not told why I was being charged. The sergeant who arrested me didn't know why he had arrested me. Furthermore, it took him five or six hours to decide,' said Black, who added he had not had a drink that night."

"Burnel said he drank only one glass of wine before police took away the bottle. He said he kept moving about and this might have misled the sergeant into thinking he was drunk. Marks said he was on his way out of the station when he was arrested for obstructing police. Magistrates refused an application for costs against the police."

On 16th November, the *Daily Mirror* reported the event in a way that made it sound far more volatile; "Punk party in the cop shop — Two members of the punk rock group The Stranglers tried to hold "a party" at a police station in the early hours of the morning, a court heard yesterday. They shouted and waved their arms about and refused to leave. One was carrying a wine bottle and drinking from a glass, Brighton magistrates were told."

The sergeant who arrested them was quoted as having said; "They were provocative — intent on holding a party in my station. Everybody was shouting abuse and taking the mickey."

Different sources gave different accounts. Regarding the arrest in Brighton, it was reported in *New Musical Express* that Jet Black hadn't been allowed to use the phone or the medicine that he needed while in custody. Black was quoted; "We're all perplexed by police activity in Brighton."

According to the bootleg at least, the audience at Hastings Pier on 29th October sound less than enthusiastic (quiet clapping rather than cheering, certainly not as rowdy as other crowds that year). Musically, The Stranglers don't play below par. It's interesting to consider how, at this stage in their tenure, they still attracted a very mixed reception. It's possible that they fed off the volatility of an audience and were maybe taken aback when some were more docile. They must have anticipated that volatility was more likely to be the order of the day. Greenfield was quoted in the *Sunday Mirror* in June; "People spit at us and throw bottles because they've got this idea that we like it."

It was reported in the *Daily Mirror* on 8th October; "In Coventry, where The Stranglers appeared last week as part of their massive forty four date British tour, they were obviously pleased that they had packed 2,400 people into Tiffany's club. But they were disappointed at the "tameness" of the audience."

To which Burnel was quoted, "Last time we were here they threw eggs. We don't like violence, but if somebody has a go we obviously have to defend ourselves."

That's not to say that The Stranglers didn't have an understanding of their audience though. Far from it in fact. The band seemed to be very aware that their music provided an outlet for the frustrations that a lot of people in the audience may have felt at the time.

Burnel told the *Sunday Mirror* in June; "Audiences get very tense and excited, because of the way life is today there are a lot of frustrated people out there, and the music gives it a chance to come to the surface."

Were The Stranglers necessarily advocating for violence for its own sake though? Cornwell told *Record Mirror* in January; "Things won't change by violence. There will be a silent revolution. There are a lot of very intelligent people around today who are fed up with our constitution. They are slowly increasing in number and something is bound to happen soon. A majority of people agree that the government has no credibility. I see my role as someone trying to make the country see that the sixty and seventy year old politicians have absolutely no contact with the public. They may start off with good intentions but, after years of crawling, they become meaningless. Like Denis Squealy, they don't want to lose what they've got. I'd like to make enough money to buy a huge mansion and put all the politicians in separate rooms so they can play with themselves."

"What we need desperately is a Robin Hood character... If music leads to violence then it ain't music anymore. The function of the artist is to express and to reflect the environment. A band should show people they are well within their rights to hold a certain view. There's no point in making things up. The artist has got to be true to his expectations. Music's function is not to create. It isn't a spark in a fuse — it's a separate entity. And what's very important about the new wave music is that the guys up on stage singing have the same problems as those watching. I'm fed up of those little schmucks who live, breathe and have the same bodily functions as everyone else, yet strive to be inaccessible. Even Rod Stewart gets diarrhoea. The new wave could be the first step towards utopia."

The gig that took place at the Village Bowl in Bournemouth on 27th October was reviewed in *Melody Maker* the following month; "In Bournemouth, the streets are under sedation, not just laid back but a pensioners' paradise — one of the first buildings I saw was a Freemasons' hall. Definitely more of a home from home for the blubbery pseudo-poetry of Rod McKuen the following night than for The Stranglers and The Dictators... The Stranglers were exhausted, having spent the whole night before wrangling with Old Bill, but they still displayed their usual aggressive enthusiasm. I'm worried about some of their songs, but not their performance of them. I've been on The Stranglers' side for a long time — you can't help but have a soft spot for a band you follow before they ever look like making it. And some of their music is undoubtedly brilliant — 'Sometimes', 'Hanging Around', 'Straighten Out' and 'Grip' in particular. But lyrically many of them express a thoroughly nasty sexism through which women become 'nubiles', mere receptacles for a man's lust — 'making love to the Mersey Tunnel with a sausage' from 'London Lady' has to be one of the most revoltingly retrogressive lines ever penned. By all means revel in their music — a lot of it is great — but for heaven's sake think carefully about what they're saying."

There seemed to be much excitement and anticipation in the build up to a Stranglers gig. It was considered in the *Reading Evening Post* on 29th October; "When The Stranglers arrive at Reading tomorrow for their Top Rank gig it will be as one of the country's top bands — if not *the* top band. They have broken attendance records set by The Rolling Stones and The Who. They have records high in the singles charts and they have gained more critical acclaim than probably any other punk band. The reason for that is, I suppose, because their music is the least punk and the most accessible of the new wavers. It has its roots in the sixties, being very similar to the sound The Doors were putting out then. Of course, The Stranglers have made many enemies along the way to stardom — who hasn't?! But really, their off-stage antics are no more disturbing than those of The Rolling Stones a decade ago."

The following feature in the *Reading Evening Post* two days later puts the spotlight on the audience, so much so that it doesn't make much reference to The Stranglers' performance. It is understandable considering all of the build-up surrounding the gig in terms of some people preparing for the worst. Ultimately, a level of violence had been anticipated that didn't actually happen. It speaks volumes perhaps, in terms of what some feared about The Stranglers and the majority of their audience compared to what the reality actually was.

"Punk rock came to Reading in a big way last night, when more than 2,000 excited fans poured into the town to be met by a "softly, softly" police operation. And the police decision to keep a low profile as hundreds of fans converged on the Top Rank Suite, paid off. There were no reports of trouble before or after the concert presented by top punk band The Stranglers. And the Top Rank management said everything went just as smoothly inside. 'It all went very well,' said manager Mr Alex Crichton, 'there was no trouble at all. Everybody was very well behaved.'

And as the fans made their way home after 11:30pm, a Reading police spokesman said 'We decided to keep a very low profile. We kept a fatherly distant eye on things and had no problems at all. We have had no reports of trouble.' Fans came from as far away as Dublin to see The Stranglers said Top Rank management. The band are fast becoming one of the biggest crowd-pullers in the country. There was even a contingent from Belgium, said the Top Rank spokesman."

"Punk fans, many attired in the traditional "uniform" of ripped clothing, dyed hair, safety pins and zippers, started packing the steps to the Top Rank well before the doors opened. Others turned up wearing baggy sweaters, bizarre makeup, and clothes held together with safety pins. Some even sported metal-studded dog collars round their necks and wore plastic sandals. There was a capacity house with nearly 2,000 people inside. More than fifty had to be turned away at the door, said Mr Crichton, but they did not make any trouble, and soon drifted off. A few minor scuffles developed on the steps before the doors opened, as pressure grew to get inside."

"Tickets were sold out days ahead, said management, and phone calls poured in all yesterday as people tried to buy up any last-minute cancellations. Groups of fans gathered near Reading station several hours before the concert was due to start, but reports said they were well behaved. Inside the Top Rank Suite, many fans appeared in a state of near collapse through the terrific heat generated on the dance floor — where hundreds of people were squashed together in a constantly surging mass. One young girl was pulled out of the crowd jammed against the edge of the stage — for her own safety as the crush moved towards her. At one time warnings were issued for fans to stay away from the lighting and sound controls on the floor — in case they disrupted the show. Special plastic glasses were used in the bars — a wise measure as they soon became missiles when fans were carried away by the pounding beat. There was little work for the Top Rank security men to do as the massed fans rocked the building with enthusiastic foot-stamping."

The Roundhouse performance on 2nd November was reported on in *New Musical Express* the same month; "Wiping his face with a towel, Hugh Cornwell snaps angrily into the mic 'We didn't come here to be spat at. It's very difficult to play when you're being spat at.' So that was why The Stranglers were playing so badly. Enthusiastically they'd opened their first show of a five-night residency at London's Roundhouse with 'No More Heroes' and then within fifteen minutes put across two of their most popular numbers, 'Bring On The Nubiles' and 'Sometimes'."

"Theoretically at least it's the type of material on which to build an excellent set, but the sound is appalling and their playing little more than amateur. It leaves the majority of the audience deflated and unimpressed and the sight of Cornwell blaming them for this dreadful performance unsurprisingly results in some harsh verbal exchanges. 'So what d'ya come for if you don't like it?' Cornwell ineffectually concludes, and without waiting for the expected reply the band launch into another number, equally as awful as the preceding one."

"Over the last year The Stranglers have emerged as the most successful recording band on the periphery of the new wave without which they might be little more than a regular chart act — a notion born out of the fact that they are seemingly one of the country's worst live acts. From playing the two albums and reading the reviews, I had anticipated seeing one of Britain's most exiting acts. And where better for them to perform than the Roundhouse, the venue where they first attracted the praise of the London press as support to Patti Smith."

"Their show should have been a triumph, a display of tremendous collective talent we had all been led to believe existed, instead it was a gloomy homecoming for four guys who played as if completely drained of inspiration. Cornwell is struggling through most of the set, his gaunt face reflecting his mixed emotions, going from anger to frustration, belligerence to violence, until eventually he is a desperate man. As he lashes at his guitar and feebly attempts to solo with erratic, brittle lines, he is a pitiful sight, and one that strangely the other three band members ignore."

"Bassist Jean-Jacques Burnel nonchalantly shimmies off to Cornwell's right, taking every other lead vocal, while Dave Greenfield keeps his eyes firmly down on his various keyboard instruments, and drummer Jet Black slugs out... nearly all night. Among other pieces they play 'Hanging Around', 'I Feel Like A Wog' and other selections from the first and second albums, and even include a new song, '5 Minutes'. But every one is a monotonous testimonial to The Stranglers' apathy, repetitive drones that insults the instrumental energy and ability they project in the studio. It hits Cornwell the hardest, who at one point tells the capacity audience (hardly any of whom appear to be punks) 'This is as quiet as being in The Red Cow on a Wednesday night — something better change.' Of course this is a cue to the song of the same name, and although it is one of their better performances does little to relieve the tedium."

"How they have the nerve to return and play two encores, 'Peaches' and 'Grip' is beyond me and it is at this desperate point Cornwell completely disgraces himself. Having derided his own fans, he now bleeds all over the stage, telling the crowd that the gig nearly didn't happen because power cuts imposed by councils. Needless to say this is fatuous and just another bullshit excuse for what is in reality and appalling show."

Could it be that the review is reflective of a bad night on the basis that The Stranglers were coming towards the tail end of the *No More Heroes* tour? Well, maybe. Or maybe journalist, Tony Parsons, wasn't a fan? Or hey, maybe they did have a bad night. Having not heard a bootleg of the gig, it is impossible to comment but notably, it highlights the importance of other bootlegs in how they provide an overall picture of what The Stranglers sounded like whilst on tour in 1977.

The bootleg of the gigs that took place and the Roundhouse on 5th and 6th November goes by the names of *London Ladies* and *Rattus Brittanicus*. Some of the tracks from these gigs were recorded and put onto the official 1979 release, *Live (X Cert)*.

It's endearing that recordings from the Roundhouse were put out as an official release considering that it was a favourite venue. Jet Black said in *Record Mirror* in August; "We lost some dates on the last tour and it was a problem trying to find alternative places to play. In our early days we were banned from Dingwalls, but we didn't really care because we hate Dingwalls. The ideal venue has to be the Roundhouse. I wish there were more places like that. About that size and where the kids can stand up — that's important for us. If the audience is seated, you lose something, the closeness. We'll be doing another British tour in September, playing more or less the same places as last time. We definitely won't be playing a string of Odeons up and down the country. It's not what we want to do."

Extra dates had to be added to the tour in order to accommodate The Stranglers' popularity. It was reported in the *Belfast Telegraph* on 18th October that a second show at Ulster Hall had been added for Wednesday 9th November "due to public demand".

In September when the *Belfast Telegraph* announced that The Stranglers would be coming to Belfast on 8th November, it was noted that "although the sight of Technicolor-haired punk rockers with their nostrils aerated with safety pins is still a rarity in Belfast, indications are that the music is gaining in popularity. Our spies in the record shops report healthy sales for new wave records, especially for The Stranglers."

The self-identified Two New Wave Fans had their letter printed in the *Belfast Telegraph* in November; "On behalf of all those who bought tickets for The Stranglers' concerts we would like to "thank" Belfast City Council and insurance companies involved for their "assistance" in enabling the concerts to take place as published. The Stranglers are one of the few who are prepared to visit Northern Ireland. The Stranglers' concert date was first published two months ago and since then over 3,000 tickets were sold — an extra gig was arranged to satisfy an overwhelming demand. There is little enough for the young people of Belfast to do, especially since the cinema bombings, and any entertainment available has age limitations. If 3,000 people in Northern Ireland are prepared to pay from £2 to £3 to see The Stranglers live this must show that many people have been influenced and impressed by them."

I guess the fact that they put the words "thank" and "assistance" in inverted commas was them having a dig at all the debate the council may have had surrounding whether or not to let the gigs go ahead, as was common throughout some boroughs in the country that year.

In the case of Belfast, it seems that there was certainly an extent of to-ing and fro-ing as to whether or not The Stranglers would be allowed to play there, as another reader's letter published in the *Belfast Telegraph* earlier in November shows: "I have just been told that The Stranglers' concerts have been cancelled. Words cannot express the anger and disappointment I feel over this issue. Live music has been a rarity in Northern Ireland during the troubles. A few weeks ago we had The Clash fiasco. The cancellation took place a few hours before it was due to begin and after many fans had already left for it. We were told The Stranglers were ninety nine percent certain to play. Why are concerts arranged in the first place without insurance cover being assured and why is it left so late to tell the fans concerts have been cancelled? The Stranglers concerts have been arranged for several months during which time there must have been ample time to check the insurance. I feel an explanation of this scandalous series of events is owed to the music fans."

It really did take a lot of doing to get a Stranglers gig up and running in Belfast. It was reported in the *Belfast Telegraph* on 21st October that the previous night's gig had been cancelled due to insurance cover being withdrawn at the last minute. The insurance company considered the risk to be too high after hearing about damage that had occurred at a gig with The Clash.

A reader's letter was published in the same paper on 15th November; "Yet another concert, that of The Stranglers, has been cancelled due to the same insurance problem. It seems that the City Council think the fans are going to demolish the hall as soon as we enter. I would like to point out, that about two years ago, when the Bay City Rollers played, considerable damage was caused, yet they have never had this insurance problem. It seems that if you wear drainpipes and play music known as "punk rock", you are classed as some kind of animal. However, this was proved wrong two weeks ago when The Runaways played and no damage was caused. Why condemn us before we've had a chance to prove ourselves? There is little enough entertainment in Northern Ireland, without taking what there is away from the young people here."

Efforts had been made to save the gigs at the last minute, but to no avail. The *Belfast Telegraph* reported on 7th November that "two punk rock concerts in Belfast tomorrow and Wednesday night have been called off. The promoters, Live and Kickin' have sent a telegram to The Stranglers telling them the shows are off because they can't get insurance cover. More than 3,000 tickets had been sold for the two concerts. Attempts to persuade insurance underwriters in Belfast, London, Dublin and France to provide public liability failed. A five-figure insurance surety which the promoters offered Belfast City Hall was rejected, according to Live and Kickin'."

The difficulty of finding venues willing to host The Stranglers was such that it had an impact on the scope of where they could tour. In terms of where the tour didn't extend to, it probably wasn't for a lack of trying, at least on the band's part.

Ian Grant of Albion management had a statement printed in *Record Mirror* on 1st October; "The Stranglers current tour is the most extensive ever undertaken by a new wave band. If we could play in Edinburgh, Aberdeen etc. we would. Unfortunately we couldn't find a venue in Edinburgh and we have been banned completely in Dundee by the Law of Provost. Aberdeen was another place that was unable to provide a suitable venue to fit in with the tour schedule. The band would like to point out they are playing places like Caernarvon in Wales and Canterbury in Kent so they are by no means sticking solely to larger venues."

On balance, not all cancellations were for the same

reasons. *Record Mirror* reported on 28th May that the Coventry date had to be cancelled due to Hugh Cornwell having the flu. It also stated that a date set for 18th June at the Blackpool Imperial Hotel had been cancelled due to a "booking mix-up" and that a gig scheduled for the Blackburn King George's Hall the following night had also been cancelled on the basis of objections from the council.

The bootleg of the gig that took place at the Hope and Anchor on 22nd November is an important recording because it shows where The Stranglers were at as a live band by the time they had two successful albums under their belt. By the time it came to playing at the small Hope and Anchor, at this point in their tenure, The Stranglers had played bigger venues. Perhaps in homage to the venue and what it had done for them at the start of their career, as well as playing almost everything from their two albums released that year, The Stranglers included some of their earlier songs in their set — 'Choosey Susie', 'Tits' and 'Mean To Me'.

A delightful homage to their earlier days considering that their setlist would be due to change again just months later with their third album on the horizon. Although the performance was released officially by EMI in 1992, it matters that there was a bootleg of it doing the rounds prior to that. Likewise the bootleg of the gig that took place at The Paradiso in Amsterdam on 27th November is a gem. The Stranglers played for two nights at this venue and this bootleg documents the first one. Back to the venue after being there just a few months earlier on the 2nd September, the set opens with 'Ugly'. Cornwell lets the audience know they are being filmed. It must have been strange times for The Stranglers considering what their time in Amsterdam was like overall.

Record Mirror reported in December; "Pass me the

aphrodisiac, honey, we're in Amsterdam. And all the cutie canal streets and all the clapperboard clubs and all the demonic deck hands of this cold Indonesian restaurant night lead to The Paradiso. Now The Paradiso is Amsterdam's premier hole. Like, imagine the Roundhouse only *dirtier* — a huge filter tip after the cigarette has gone, the death brown fusing of nicotine, tar, spit all the way through. That's The Paradiso. Then you look up way above the stage. Stained glass windows are the only clue that this was once a church. Yeah that's right, a church."

"Now there's a dope bar where the font used to be, kids snort in the shadow of the altar and The Stranglers replace Christ. Hey, is that a tear on the multi-coloured cheek of Mary up there? 'Christ he told his mother, Christ he told her not to bother.' There's a thousand punters inside, another thousand outside and a Dutch TV film unit celluloiding the lot. The Stranglers — high-rise exponents of the kinda devout decadence inherent in pre-war Berlin."

"They always remind me of a scene in *The Thief Of Baghdad* when a wealthy Indian merchant fell in love with a life-size mechanical doll with eight arms. He paid a fortune for it and then indulged in some Eastern delight. The doll had huge fingernails and it proceeded to dig then into his back as he held it. Slowly and sex-sadistically at first, then harder until the blood seeped out and he died. Think about it. There's something very unclean about The Stranglers. I always feel like taking a shower after seeing them. Their phenomenal success among the pre-pubes baffles me. They have no obvious attraction for that particular strata as far as I can see. What thirteen year old has ever heard of Trotsky?"

"They ain't too glamorous. Their clothes are straight out of a Black Sabbath queue of fans. They don't exactly come on like teenies. 'What did you do in the war, daddy?'

the far-out, bombed-out, bleached-out (I'll refrain from saying 'cop-out' cause I don't think that's entirely correct) fall out that is The Stranglers somehow get across to them. Like dirty old men offering sweets to little girls. Same applied to this spaced-out Dutch-capped Paradiso audience. They ain't got the faintest idea about what the band are going on about but they cheer every familiar chord. The show is their usual sex act taking the boots off. One new song, '5 Minutes', indicates a variation but the tried and trusted format is the same. Why change success? That's what the proles seem to want, so give it to 'em good. Fact is I enjoy their shows, their records, their pose. It may be really cool to slag them for writing anti-feminist songs (though I thought that most songs professing to be "love" songs were anyway. Writers from Porter to Lennon have regarded women as merely love objects, gossamer fantasies in men's minds) or for making dough but their desirability rating is high in my estimation. I'm down to ten a day now. They bring out the prurience in people — and that can't be all bad."

The feature continued: "Now we get to the meat of the story. Halfway through 'Ugly' just before the 'It's only the children of the fucking wealthy that tend to be good looking' bit a kid jumps on stage and dances. A security guard casually strolls on and hurls the kid off stage. Nothing out of the ordinary you might say. But the guard was a Hell's Angel, built like a prefab and the stage happens to be eight foot off the ground. Burnel stops playing and tells the Angel to cool it. But that's all he can do. The Angel politely and begrudgingly nods. The first taste of what's going to happen on this acerbic Amsterdam evening."

"The band finish the number and the rest of the show runs relatively smoothly with only the slightest hint of Angel cakewalking sidestage. The Dutch Angels have muscled their way into The Stranglers' camp. Whenever they play Holland the Angels are there offering friendly advice and bicep service. The band like them, there's no doubting that. But it wouldn't much matter if they didn't. See the Hell's Angels of Amsterdam are different from their counterparts in Britain, America or Timbuktu. They're government approved! No kiddin'. The Dutch Government allocated a £150,000 grant to enable the Amsterdam Hell's Angels Society, as it's officially known, to set up shop. With that money, the Society built an Angel complex on the city's outskirts."

"It includes a large clubhouse complete with disco and bar, sleeping quarters, a garage to house their 1000cc steeds and a makeshift shooting range. And, wait for it, each of the Society's twenty five members receives an annual grant of £2,000. Altogether now. *Why?* Fear appears to be the prime motivation for such an insane policy. It seems the government are afraid of this happy band of men and the money is merely a ruse to keep them quiet. A do-it-yourself-Nazi-jacketed protection racket. It's on the government maaan!"

"Backstage after the show The Stranglers enjoy a spot of quiet relaxation with their new found buddies. I get some long, ludicrous, electric-drill-in-the-kneecaps stare from one of the Angels as I walk into the dressing room. 'He's all right' says Hugh. His timing was just right. The Indonesian meal I had stuffed down earlier was ready to make an unscheduled appearance on the floor. 'They took us back to their clubhouse after we played last night,' he continues 'I stayed until six this morning. They gave us anything we wanted. They treated us like kings.' Hugh is clearly loving every Evel Knievel moment of it. Dave sits nearby cuddling his missus. Jet surveys. Jean has vanished. 'He's gone to pick up his motorbike. We're going back to the club again tonight.' Says Hugh. Oh great."

Still from the same feature: "It was somewhere between the b in club and the a in again when the loudest banger you've ever heard went off at my feet. A group of three bearded (ain't they all) Angels chuckle in the corner. 'You come with us ya?' 'Er, well if it's all the same to you I'll go in the van with the band.' The last time The Stranglers played here the boize took them along to a pleasant little bar slap bang in the middle of the red-light district. Their birds are whores who pop up in between grovelling clients for a sociable drink. But this time it's da bizness. The Angel Club. The building is well away from residents' areas. One of the government's stipulations I guess. But there is a prison, a rather tall luxury block (well you know what these permissive countries are like about crime) under construction nearby. 'They'll never finish that prison,' a visiting Brighton Angel casually informs me as we drive past. 'The communists don't want it so they keep bombing the place every now and then'."

"There's also another reason why the building won't be completed for some time. In the back garden of the club is a large, mounted machine gun. When an Angel fancies some fun he strolls out back, loads up the gun and sends hails of bullets through the prison windows. Cute huh. Inside it's tastefully lit, that's probably 'cos most of the bulbs have been smashed maybe. Hugh plays pool with a guy affectionately referred to as 'Loser'. His face has been eaten away by the acid shower he got in a bundle. Halfway through the game the barman starts showing home movies. Well, they can't be that bad if they make those cosy family films. Why look, isn't that this very same club? And isn't that the pool table that Hugh's on. How sweet. Oh look, there's a a..... er.... *gulp*..... naked lady! Giggles at the bar. 'Look that's me hahahahaha.' And sure enough it is. He's holding a milk bottle which he rams roughly into the bird. 'She was a German girl who wanted to be shown round,' whispers Loser in my ear. They certainly showed her everything. Then there's film of two Kraut Angels who got stroppy. They're dragged back to the club, searched at stern gunpoint and their weapons confiscated. Big Al the President of the Society tells them to get outta town and they plod mournfully offscreen. Or how about the guy with the ginger beard in the cowboy hat acting the fool in the film. Loser says he's in a lunatic asylum. When the lights come on after the show there's that same guy drinking beer at the bar."

"A few fancy revs and in comes Jean on his Triumph bike along with an Angel on his multi-million pound Harley Davidson. Jean's mascara is smudged but he still retains his cucumber cool. Why the stunt? Little Bob Hart from *The Sun* is doing a feature on The Stranglers/ Motorbikes/Hell's Angels/Dross and his photographer has set up a contrived but nevertheless effective happy snap. The Angels indulge in a spot of frantic posing. Stranglers posing comes naturally anyway and the shot has more than a passing similarity to one of those Barry Sheene victory scenes after a world championship race."

"After the session Hart drags Jean into a room for an interview, Hugh continues playing pool, Jet continues drinking and Dave continues to cuddle his missus. This guy in a balaclava comes wandering over to where publicist Alan Edwards and me sit. 'Good yah. It is point twenty-two calibre. Powerful for such a little gun yah.' 'Oh yah yah' says Alan visibly quaking. Balaclava Billy or whatever wanders off. 'Bet it wasn't loaded' says Alan. The photographer walks in. 'Here they're all shooting bottles off walls with revolvers out the back.' I ask Big Al if they have problems with the police. 'The police? Hahahaha.

They never come here. They're too scared.' What about licences for their shooters. 'Hahahah.' He gives me his card *Amsterdam Society of Hell's Angels. President Big Al. Vice President Stanley.*"

"As we leave the Angels shake our hands and tell us we're welcome at any time. With every shake I keep thinking a knife's gonna go in my back. That ice cream soft entry comblike parting of the flesh, the rose red spill, the midnight walk thump thump of the heart, the dirty steel caressing the bone before breaking it, the cool call of death. I got to thinking about newspaper headlines 'Pop group and friends slaughtered by Hell's Angels'. Of only the good die young sentiments. Of bright future epitaphs, of me mum and dad, me bird. A hand hits me on the back. 'Goodnight. Safe journey.' Phew."

"In the van, Jean gives me his spiel about how he's got this coloured motorbike prodigy. 'He's gonna be a world champion. He's great, and he's *black* man!' He goes on to discuss the Triumph motorcycle factory and how cooperatives don't work and a whole host of other such riveting subjects at Peter O'Sullivan breakneck vocal speed. 'See you later.' So I'm left to think about the night. And you know what I think? I think the Angels are nice guys in their way, but their way ain't my way. The government pay them to keep schtum and out of the limelight. The Stranglers, unintentionally, have brought them out of automaton abeyance. They ain't thugs but they ain't exactly pussycats either."

"A few people have mentioned unpleasant scenes they witnessed on the band's last British tour involving some of the Angels. Remember Altamont? Maybe that sounds a little drastic but it's not just the Angels you gotta worry about. It's the ordinary punters reaction as well. While The Stranglers keep insisting on playing smaller venues there's always the danger of violence. Playing a place the size of The Paradiso ain't fair on the fans or the band. Christ they could pack out the Empire Pool two nights in a row now, maybe even three. Slapdash security just ain't good enough anymore. Nice gesture sure but something better change quick. Whatever happened to... The Finchley Boys?"

An amount of the language and overall attitudes towards women and black people expressed in the article are very much of their time. It just goes to show that in context, if The Stranglers' observational lyrics did make people uncomfortable, they were very much a product of their time. Some events described sound frankly, terrifying. It raises a question in terms of, were certain details enhanced or fabricated by the journalist in order to play up to The Stranglers' public image, or was life on the road with them really that dangerous?

We'll probably never know the full details without having been a fly on the wall but considering that violence did happen at some of their gigs, the company they were in may have possibly felt normal to them at the time. Notably, the report was done by Barry Cain who seemed to have a good rapport with The Stranglers — not something to be underestimated considering the distain that the band had for a lot of the media at the time. Cain's rapport with The Stranglers must have been a healthy one considering that he attended the unveiling of their PRS plaque in Guildford in January 2019 at the Star Inn.

Hanging out with the Hell's Angels was familiar territory to Burnel, he had been doing so in the days before The Stranglers. He told *Shews*; "I also nearly fucked up my A-Levels because I was riding my motorbike every night because I was going to places around Walton-on-Thames — rock 'n' rolling down places like Hersham, which was a working men's club, then we used to go down there and every Friday night all the motorcycle gangs used to turn up and teds as well. There were Walton Hell's Angels, Windsor Hell's Angels, The Nightingales, Hell's Angels England, and a lot of other gangs. When they'd all come up on their bikes, there would be about two hundred bikes there."

Burnel was probably less frightened of the events in Amsterdam than many would have been. Regarding the Hell's Angels, he told *New Musical Express* in October; "They dress filthy but their bikes *gleam*, their bikes are spotless – and their women look even fiercer than they do! The Angels we met from Holland live in their own exclusive community in Amsterdam and they don't have to worry about working for a living because all their women are *on the game*! They're able to devote all their time to their bikes. It's great. They've created a totally new society."

So which venues were The Stranglers' favourite ones to perform at? According to Jet Black talking to *Sideburns* in January; "We are not into the idea of touring around the country playing venues in excess of our drawing capacity... We like the kind of venue where you can see the whites of their eyes. Hammersmith Odeon isn't so good in that sense, but the Roundhouse is more suitable because you can really see the audience in front of you... We've got mixed feelings about the Marquee, it doesn't seem to be where it's all at – at the moment the Nashville is a far more enjoyable gig to play for some strange reason."

It seems that on the gigging front, London was The Stranglers' first love. Greenfield told *Zigzag* in November '76; "London's fantastic to work. There's real concentrated awareness which hits us. You get really nice audiences who understand the music."

Burnel in the same feature said; "Everywhere we play outside London we go down like a fart in a church because they're expecting old fashioned music. It seems you've got to wear huge stiletto heels and play heavy lead guitar all the time. I can't understand it. People seem to need some sort of starting point to identify or compare a band. They don't know where to categorise us. What we are doing with The Stranglers is different for this country at least. If we are, as a lot of people are saying, psychedelically orientated, we don't deny it. It's just a new departure for this country. We're taking over where other bands left off years ago, and we're opening the floodgates for other groups too."

However, Burnel was quoted in *Strangled* saying; "London audiences have become intolerant and cliques — self destructive, the lemming syndrome."

Even after a year of tumultuous touring dramas, in 1977 The Stranglers had made it, albeit very much in their own way. It was considered in the *Aberdeen Evening Express* in December; "In February I watched The Stranglers being showered with beer glasses (albeit plastic ones) at the McRobert Hall in Aberdeen. The music they played — which put them into the single and album charts — would undoubtedly win them an ovation now. Before the show really got on the road, what the country north of London was being fed was unimpressive. But how things have changed. Perhaps it hasn't been the most commercially viable breakthrough but it is established, something I couldn't see a year ago."

Were the dramas of touring all part and parcel of what was on trend in 1977? Some would certainly say so. It was considered in the *Coventry Evening Telegraph* in December; "Whatever happened to the pop scene's Mr Nice Guy during 1977? It was a year when wholesome, clean-cut artists very much played second fiddle in the popularity stakes to the outrageous punks. Rebellion became a key word during '77 as the race to out-shock and out-swear hotted up. But haven't we seen it all before? Since the day Bill Haley first rocked around the clock, youth has been finding music a way of hitting out at the establishment, authority, society and the elder generation. Today's punk heroes, Johnny Rotten and his Sex Pistols, The Stranglers, Richard Hell, Billy Idol, The Clash and the Boomtown Rats have chosen names to outrage. So what's new? British rock twenty years ago brought us the likes of Billy Fury, Marty Wilde and Vince Eager. Their manager, Larry Parnes, did his best to stimulate parental ridicule, thus ensuring his stars had an identity with youth, by renaming them with emotional surnames."

That reporter gets it. As much as the music itself was important and is what has really stood the test of time, clever manipulations were plausibly employed to create a sense of controversy where there would otherwise not have been one.

Chapter Five

A Legacy

The extent of The Stranglers' success in 1977 was well documented in the *Daily Mirror* in the October of that year; "In the grip of The Stranglers — Gone are the days when The Stranglers crammed into their ice cream van to take them to bookings where they were booed off stage. After eighteen months of everybody telling them they'd never get anywhere except nowhere, they finally made it big — just in time. They didn't have much money left in the kitty and the ice cream van was about to collapse on them."

"In less than a year The Stranglers have sold £750,000 worth of records and are probably the most sought-after of the new wave bands. They deny that overnight success has changed their lives. Being at the top means a takeaway kebab after yet another late-night gig and a lift home in someone's van. Instead of taking a fiver a night each home from a date they just pocket fifty pounds a week from what they are making now. Guitarist and lead singer Hugh Cornwell and bass guitarist Jean-Jacques Burnel are of no fixed abode at the moment. They don't feel the need for a permanent home. Money, it would seem, is almost a dirty word. They appear to be concerned only that they punter gets a fair deal."

Tour manager Dick O'Dell was quoted in the same feature; "Their potential is limitless. It is difficult to say

161

exactly what they are worth at the moment."

The Stranglers' potential was evident to many, even before they became a household name. A gig that took place at the Marquee on 7th November 1976 was reviewed the same month in *New Musical Express*; "'We'd like to mourn the death of the Marquee. The place is dead. The regulars have grown into the wallpaper, the Marquee don't know what's going on today. Wait till we've finished then smash the place up.' Hugh Cornwell, guitar player with The Stranglers, looks old even by my standards, yet whenever he opens his mouth he spews forth kindergarten nihilist polemics, the sort of immature garbage you can smile at when lisped by babes like Rat Scabies or Barrie Masters — but from a grown up recycling Doors licks, well, it's just sad."

"And when he's doing it he's on stage at the Marquee, striving desperately to join the Pistols in getting banned from there — when it's the Marquee that launched unquestionably the most successful of all punk affiliated bands (that's still what The Hot Rods are) — it's plain stupid. Despite their verbal idiocy, which seems also to run through their songs, The Stranglers are pretty certain to be huge. The fact is they are a terrific band."

"Every member is a strong player: Jet Black (strangely enough the central motif of one of their best songs, 'Down In The Sewer', reminds me of Jet Harris/Tony Meehan kitsch instrumental cinemascope) is good and energetic, but he can hit that Mo Tucker metronome when required; Jean-Jacques Burnel may be a lousy singer — but some of his bass work — particularly on a rather childish anti-education tirade embellished with discipline fantasies called 'School Man' (sic) — is authoritative enough to act as lead. Dave Greenfield enacts his Ray Manzarek duties with aplomb, his astute use of piano and organ both as colour, as lead and as play-off against the guitar is a joy to hear, and he throws in an ok Dracula type vocal on 'You're Not Real', while Cornwell is fine as a singer and breaks up his Velveteen riffing with lovely flowing Robby Krieger leads."

"On just hearing them live, their words leave something to be desired. 'London Lady' for instance appears to be a regressively sexist rock 'n' roll put down, while 'Bitching', a rant against everything in general and "posers" in particular, ill befits a mob of would-be 1966 LA hoodlums. But the music, which fuses the Velvets with The Doors, and the songs, which are dynamically structured with a sophistication quite alien to the minimalist bands who are the only comparable phenomenon to The Stranglers around these days, have a drive and a flair that is quite intoxicating. 'Go Buddy Go' is a hit. The boring thing is that their conformist "rebel" image will require them to smash up the dressing room when they appear on *Top Of The Pops*." (as it just so happens, Burnel would go on to do this exact thing at a later date!)

The latter review makes it clear that comparisons to The Doors (and indeed, the Velvet Underground) were there in abundance from The Stranglers' early days. In an interview with *Shews* in 1977, Burnel talked of his love for The Doors. "I reckon that they were about the only rock band I ever listened to, there wasn't much else."

Influences aside though, the journalist's prediction about the success that was to come was certainly a fair assessment. It suggests that The Stranglers had star quality even before they rose to fame in 1977. What Cornwell is reported to have said at the start of the gig captures the sardonic style that would stay with The Stranglers for years to come when addressing their audience. It's fascinating to think that it had been there since the early days and they didn't temper it once they became more of a high profile band.

1977 was a good year for The Stranglers in the sense that artistically they were all on the same page. That's something of an achievement considering all those who were against them that year (maybe that in itself was a bonding experience for the band – an "us versus them" mentality).

It was considered in *Sounds* in September that "a quick look on the label of a Stranglers record will credit no one individual with songwriting credits. The experienced ear can often pick out individual authorship (except from the man from the NME who thought Hugh Cornwell was responsible for the voice as well as the lyrics of 'Princess Of The Streets') but the songs as such are conceived by the band as a whole."

"Sitting in the dressing room, riding in the car, playing in the studio, they pick up on phrases in conversation and marry them to a riff or beat someone has in their heads. New numbers are normally rehearsed at soundchecks but if nothing seems to be working out after twenty minutes or so, that number is dumped unceremoniously. A hard system perhaps, and one that might trample on a few egos from time to time. But it is one which makes The Stranglers an unusually cohesive band. The strength of purpose carries over on to record. Few have failed to notice the actual sound of The Stranglers. It's full, round and rich in texture."

When asked if there were many arguments within The Stranglers, Burnel told *Shews*; "No. Well I have knocked Hugh out twice. That's about it really. It's just because we dig each other so much. I gave Hugh a black eye a couple of months back. Because there's this thing when you're very close to someone, you niggle each other sometimes and you're really sensitive to each other, you go out a lot together. It's not just gigs and that sort of thing. I beat Hugh up once in Portobello Road. I had three quid, right, and that was all the money I had in those days. We were taking a tape to Virgin at the time. Anyway, we passed this shop, and there was this t-shirt there that I wanted to buy and I was staring at it and Hugh was saying 'Look, you can't afford it,' and that sort of thing 'cos we had no money. I was saying 'I gotta have that t-shirt!' He was telling me not to be stupid about it and that I couldn't have it. But I kept on saying 'I gotta have that shirt, I gotta have that shirt.' He was nagging me and I told him not to. He kept on at me, and I said, 'Hugh, don't say another word, okay.' And he did, so, I went and hit him. I felt so bad, 'cos we didn't go to Virgin that day."

Comedy gold! When a friend gives you a caring and helpful bit of advice, you should definitely beat them up!

Whilst most of the punters were only too pleased to welcome The Stranglers to the stage, the media were perhaps more scathing on the basis that they pretty much revelled in the controversy from the likes of other bands such as the Sex Pistols. Equally though, there must have been times when The Stranglers were a frightening band to be in the presence of. So much so that it wasn't uncommon for Burnel to take on members of the audience that he took a dislike to. Sometimes The Stranglers' volatility extended to how they responded to other bands. Burnel said; "We got banned at Dingwalls and we were told that they received fifty three letters of complaint. That night in particular we were over the top. We smashed the support band's equipment up. Their gear was brand new this, brand new that. They were all guys with long hair, playing new synthesisers and new Gibsons. We only had a two-hundred-watt PA. In those days we used to spit at the audience quite a bit, this was about a year ago. The thing is, just because you're not known, people don't want to even listen to you. They don't believe you've got anything to say, unless you've gone through the normal hype channels."

In recent years, Burnel has made it clear in interviews that he is no longer the person he was back in the seventies when his actions contributed towards The Stranglers' reputation as an aggressive and violent band. He has stipulated that being bullied for being French was a strong catalyst for him being quick to react excessively to the smallest of incidents and that over time, he has found discipline and peace through karate. He is no longer, as he put it, a "violent little sod with a chip on my shoulder."

He was quoted in *Louder Than War* in March 2011; "We had a good time of course. I'm a completely different person now to what I was then but I had a great time. I exploited my situation to the maximum. It would be pretty sad if I was trying to be the same geezer. If anything you acquire knowledge and learn to disseminate it. You learn what to like and what to not like and how to react and not react in certain situations. You learn to negotiate with people differently, you get smarter and hopefully develop a sensibility and develop certain responsibilities towards other human beings... People say you should never regret anything but there was one kid whose lights I punched out during the *No More Heroes* tour. At that time we refused to sign autographs and one kid insisted over and over backstage. We would always let people backstage and hang out and he kept on insisting on an autograph and I went *boff* and punched him and I felt that was maybe a bit unnecessary. At that time I was on a short fuse and drugs – maybe speeding."

He was quoted in *The Quietus* in March 2014; "I've a

few regrets but nothing fundamental. I probably would've beaten up a few less people; I feel bad about that."

It wasn't always the case that The Stranglers were the aggressors. It was reported in *New Musical Express* in January; "In the early hours of last Sunday morning, the Roxy Club, London's punk watering hole, plus Saturday night attraction The Stranglers, got ripped off to the tune of the best part of a grand. After the fun was over and everybody had gone home, Roxy manager and two friends were waiting for the band's three roadies to load the equipment into the van out in Neal Street when four characters decked out to resemble refugees from *The Sweeney* appeared on the scene, two of them going straight into the Roxy and the other two approaching the road crew and saying 'into the club please, we're police officers'."

"The "cops" flashed their wallets, showing a card with Metropolitan Police embossed on the crest with white background and both roadies, Andy and friends were taken into the Roxy and none too politely ushered into Andy's eight-by-four office. The Stranglers' chief roadie tried to go downstairs to collect his briefcase containing the takings from the previous night's RCA gig, *plus* the band's emergency float — in other words, practically everything they got. The roadie was stopped by the "cops", searched and thrown back in the room before he could get the money. When Andy refused to sit down quietly in a position where he would not be able to see what the "cops" were getting up to in the foyer, they forcibly bundled him into a chair. The "cops" took the door keys from Andy and then locked the door from the outside after partaking in a none-too-convincing spate of "cop" talk."

"By now it was apparent that the "cops" weren't cops at all — just professional rip-off merchants. The plasterboard wall to the Roxy kitchen was kicked in, somebody scrambled through and released the remaining five locked in the office and within seconds the *real* cops were called — although it was too late to save the briefcase containing the takings of the recent Stranglers gigs, plus their float, a total of six hundred pounds, *plus* two hundred quid that the Roxy had taken at the door. When the police arrived they showed Andy and the others what a real identification card looked like, as opposed to the ones the hoods were carrying — and it seems that it would pay us *all* to find out what a *real* police I.D. card looks like while we get these thieves in the street."

Despite the commercial success The Stranglers were enjoying in 1977, it is apparently the case that the band themselves didn't necessarily reap the rewards of that. Overheads relating to travel and equipment were a factor but in later years, Cornwell explained that the management very much took the lion's share of the profit to the point that it may have been unreasonable. Not only were The Stranglers kept so busy with gigging that they had little time to grasp what was going on financially but also, in instances where losses were made on tour, they came out of the band's wages.

It is worth noting that there were times when The Stranglers may have felt manipulated by the media. In later years Cornwell described how he would be interviewed by journalists who would sometimes lull him into a false sense of security, so much so that he would leave the interview thinking it had gone well only to find that once it had been printed, he had been depicted in way that had been spun into something negative.

It must have been very alienating at times. It is understandable as to why The Stranglers had a low opinion of the majority of journalists. It is possible that the band might have made a rod for their own backs in some ways though, notably right from the start. Burnel said in *Zigzag* in November 1976; "We're clean wholesome boys. Just like the boys next door — if you happen to live next door to a morgue!"

The way in which some journalists were disparaging of The Stranglers continued way beyond 1977. In *New Musical Express* in January 1981, journalist Lynn Hanna wrote, "I tell Hugh Cornwell that a lot of women, including myself, found the lyrics on the first two Stranglers albums threatening and offensive. Cornwell, adopting a lofty air of detachment replies blandly, 'I'm surprised you found them threatening. Maybe that demonstrates your own insecurity'."

In response to the question of "But women aren't secure from violence are they?"

Cornwell: "That shows that a lot of women are insecure."

Her response: "Yes, but you were playing on those insecurities."

Cornwell: "Not at all, I was playing on my guitar."

Later in the interview, upon being asked about the lyrics in 'Sometimes', Cornwell said; "That was a particular situation where the girl is unfaithful and the guy reacts violently. It happens all the time. It's just a document of life."

In fairness to Cornwell's response, it was consistent with the fact that The Stranglers stated in many interviews that their lyrics were observational. Whilst the frankness of their observations may have made uncomfortable and even offensive listening for some, it is certainly the case that others found this extent of raw honesty to be refreshing.

That element of The Stranglers' music is quite punk

in its approach — that whole thing of saying things as they are. No bollocks. No fluff. Just blunt honesty, even when other people might not like it. That said, those who anticipated that punk's popularity in the mainstream would be short lived were not wrong. By the early eighties, ska and two tone were at the top of the tree.

At the end of 1977, The Stranglers went to Bearshanks Lodge in Oundle to start work on what would be their third album, *Black And White*. It would have been a different experience for them in view of the fact that unlike with *Rattus Norvegicus* and *No More Heroes*, they no longer had a few years' worth of polished material to put down on record.

Not only this, but personnel changes at United Artists resulted in a different team being formed when Andrew Lauder left. Added to this, The Stranglers grew concerned that Albion's interest in them was waning. Having worked so hard in 1977, by 1978, a feeling of cynicism was starting to creep in regarding how long the band could keep going. Burnel told *New Musical Express* in September 1978; "The lifespan of this group is very limited. It works twice as hard as any other group around. It's bound to burn itself out quickly. The Stranglers could split up at any time. It probably won't last all that much longer. After all, there's lots of other things I'd like to do. I'd like to go to Japan and study for my black belt. I don't really consider myself as a musician as such. It's not work, this, is it? It's just good play. I won't exactly be looking out for a gig after The Stranglers."

Once The Stranglers were comfortably ticking along in the mainstream of popular music, 1978 saw them make an appearance on BBC's *Rock Goes To College*. By this point though, they still seemed to present themselves as having an anti-establishment attitude. In such regard, their appearance on the show proved to be something less than a highlight in their career.

Their propensity for self-destruction was certainly no secret. It was reported in *Sounds* in October 1978; "Rattus Extinctus?... The Stranglers continued their lemming-like rush towards commercial oblivion last week when they walked out of the telerecording of the Beeb's *Rock Goes To College* at Surrey University in Guildford after just fifteen minutes of their show. Hugh Cornwell and Jean-Jacques Burnel spent the greater part of their brief set berating their student audience as 'elitist' in language that can be best described as 'street credible'."

"When the audience took umbrage to this tirade of abuse the band stormed offstage, Jet Black pausing just long enough to perform a mini-tribute to Keith Moon on his drum kit. The students union has condemned the band and notified the college rock circuit of the dangers of hiring these academic deviationists. The Beeb for its part abandoned the show and closed yet another television door on the band. There's now scarcely a slot open for the boys on the box as they've already blotted their copy book (not to mention their dressing room) on *Top Of The Pops*. Any producer must now consider them as a "high risk investment" as far as programming is concerned."

"So where does that leave the new wave band that can outsell virtually all its contemporaries in the record shops but can't or won't get through to a mass audience and can't even lure its own fans in sufficient quantities to judge from the low turn-out at their Battersea bash? Hell bent on self-destruction, that's where."

"Not only are the band shouting at their audiences, they're also bickering with their management. Cornwell and Burnel are working on solo albums (Burnel's already finished his) and optimism about the band's future is pretty hard to find around their camp at the moment. Burnel's reported as saying of their Guildford escapade: 'I suppose it's commercial suicide'. Suicide is le mot juste. Just a few weeks ago Burnel was saying gleefully that nobody was big enough to break up The Stranglers. He's right, they can do it themselves."

It is understandable as to why some TV shows preferred to play it safe and not play host to The Stranglers. It was reported in *Record Mirror* in '77; "The Stranglers have been banned from appearing on Thames Television children's show, *Magpie*. A *Magpie* spokesperson said, 'There are many groups in existence who are genuinely trying to make their way in the music jungle. Normally we would reflect the interests of these groups on *Magpie*, but while the image of new wave groups seems to be lumped with the punk rock Sex Pistols scene, *Magpie* has to guard its own image and refrain from featuring any bands with any links to the Pistols, however tenuous."

"Hopefully when the ballyhoo has died down the programme can return to its normal job of reflecting what is new and interesting in the pop scene.' Dave Greenfield, The Stranglers' keyboards player said, 'If they take things much further they are not going to have any groups at all on the show. You might as well ban all the bands that appear on *The Hughie Green Show* because they play guitars'."

When it comes to the Sex Pistols, there were times when The Stranglers were made out to be guilty by association, which is a real shame really considering that musically, both groups were very different. For instance, were the Sex Pistols ever a likely candidate to, just a few years later, be making an iconic record like 'Golden Brown', with its complex use of time signatures and emotive melody?

Overall, The Stranglers were a separate entity from their peers even from their earlier days. Regarding the Ramones, Cornwell said in *Zigzag* in November 1976; "They should stick to playing tennis. They can't play music. They have never seen a motorbike in their lives. They're Manhattan Island kids trying to be Bronx kids. We blew them off stage at the Roundhouse."

And in *Record Mirror* in January he said; "Sex Pistols — they opened the floodgates. They must be credited for that. The Damned — feel they're a bit lightweight but they have a couple of really good numbers. Eddie and The Hot Rods — even more lightweight than The Damned. Feelgoods — very good at what they do, but they've got to come up with some new material quick. The Clash — very exciting. Queen — prefer Her Majesty. Saw them on TV at Christmas and they were crap. Also at Hyde Park, or rather saw lots of flashing lights and bangs, but they weren't bad. Still, if you gave the Pistols that sort of equipment they could come up with something just as good."

The following information is technical stuff that is truthfully, beyond my understanding, but it is certainly something worth archiving here because it is important. In September '77, *Melody Maker* listed The Stranglers' musical equipment as follows:

Jet Black — Gretsch Kit: Two 20-inch bass drums. One 16x16 floor Tom Tom, 13x9 and 12x16 mounted Tom Toms, Premier bass pedal, cymbals by Zildjian and Avedis, Ludwig 6½ concert snare. Tama straight cymbal stands. Harp head streamhizer (amplifying for drums).

Hugh Cornwell — Two Fender Telecasters. Rotasound strings. Marshall 50 amplifier, heavy duty Marshall 4x12 cab.

Jean-Jacques Burnel — Fender percussion bass. Rotasound strings 4x12 cab with JBL speakers.

Dave Greenfield — Hammond L100 organ, Hohner cembalett piano (very old model, dropped from production ten years ago). A six channel Marshall mini-mixer. Two H&H slave amps, drive 2 acoustic 20's. Both keyboards direct inject into the mixing deck not mixed up, two phasers MXR phase 100 on organ and phase 90 on piano. Mini Moog to be used for the first time on upcoming tour.

The Stranglers had worked hard to get the point where they had good equipment. Jet Black said in *Sideburns* in January; "We suffered with bad equipment because we started with nothing, and we had to find the money to get equipment together. It takes a long while to get the money together if you're not working during the day, which we never did because we always believed that the way to do it was to keep playing at all costs, so that we'd become tight and develop all the time."

With all the work The Stranglers put into things, were there any regrets about not trying to crack America in the same way that they had done with the UK? According to Burnel when talking to *Louder Than War* in March 2011: "At one point we were the biggest selling band in the UK, bigger than The Clash and the Pistols. Those bands did the smart thing — like The Police and a few other bands like Flock Of Seagulls, all these bands decided to go round America until you break it. The Clash started wearing Stetsons and cowboy boots, but we could never sound American. We had American influences, I mean one big influence was The Doors of course — a blues band with an edge but we were very much a British band and America didn't suit us."

So were The Stranglers for or against the musical establishment that they had been keen to avoid being part of when they started out? According to the following article, it's anyone's guess whereby the journalist used a rather unique writing style: there are loads of comments put in brackets as if to create a to and fro sort of dialogue examining the opposing opinions that people had regarding The Stranglers, who they really appealed to and the actual scale of their success. The juxtapositions are interesting to observe (if not overly sarcastic in some places!)

Under the title of "Stranglers — Are they stinking rich, or still on the breadline?", the *Record Mirror* article in October said; "So Hugh Cornwell lives in a hole in the wall? And Jean-Jacques Burnel is homeless? Boo-hoo. Pity. Still they can keep themselves warm at night thinking of all those greenbacks heading for their carefully ripped pockets (ooh you cynic you). *Well*, what a load of crap. They'll be rich men by Christmas. *Rattus Norvegicus* has gone gold, i.e. £300,000 worth of record sales. The new album, *No More Heroes*, has already gone silver. The last single made the top twenty in four European countries and the current single jumped again to number thirteen in Britain this week. Their records sell like Wonderloaf during the bread strike, only twice as fast."

"The manager's just bought a yacht. They are punk gone *big business.* (Hold on. The manager hasn't just bought a yacht, that's gossip. They still talk to the fans). Rubbish. They've got bodyguards now. You can't get close to them. They think they're stars. Big shots. (Don't be unfair. When you've got a couple of hundred fans banging on the door after every gig you simply can't see them all. And I saw Jean-Jacques down the Vortex without a bodyguard in sight the other week). Obnoxious little chauvinist creep that he is. And those bass lines, well they were fun at first, but so limited. (Well what do you expect — the fans like it). The fans — hah. Weekend middle class punks who keep their *Rattus Norvegicus* next to their collection of ethnic jewellery and copies of *New Statesman*."

"The stinking mass market. Jesus, the huge current tour is nearly sold out already, there's been nothing like it since the Stones. (It's a good thing to reach the widest audiences possible isn't it? Otherwise it's just elitism, reverse snobbery. And touring doesn't make money per se. They have to pay money for more equipment so fans can hear better, new lighting. And are sticking to small gigs as much as possible)."

"It doesn't change the fact that they're filthy stinking rich hypocrites, mouthing 'Something Better Change' and quoting Trotsky on one hand, taking another glass of Dom Perignon from the record company advance with the other. (Actually, they didn't get a very big advance from United Arists, and they are apparently very frugal with how they use it. What's more, it takes a helluva long time to make it big in rock 'n' roll even for The Stranglers. They only get between seven to eleven percent of the record sales, and they have to pay tax on that, and then fork out for roadies, equipment, managers, PR, and God knows what else. Not forgetting that Britain is still a tiny market compared to America and The Stranglers have hardly made a dent in the charts there). I still don't think the new album's very good (There, you have a point)."

New Musical Express in October reported that "The Stranglers are well on the route to becoming the seventies equivalent of The Rolling Stones — as wantonly offensive, as grossly immoral, as *that*, as universally idolised, as outrageously successful, as affluent and establishment as *that*."

In 1977, The Stranglers seemed to be making a point

that wasn't just keen to question the musical establishment, but the societal one too. Cornwell told *Record Mirror* in January; "I used to know an armed robber. He shot someone once. I asked him about it and he said, 'Look, if someone is stupid enough to get in the way then I'm gonna stop them.' And he's right 'cos the only one who's gonna lose out is the bank. All it will mean if he gets away is one ounce of caviar less a week. People have got this weird idea that if they see a robbery they have got to stop the thief. What they should do is try and help him escape. The guy's not going to keep his hand. He'll spread it around. This country ain't poor. If people can spend fifty grand on a flat then we can't be broke. I couldn't be a bank robber though. I don't like being on the run..."

Rebellious stuff! So, with the power of hindsight, just how punk were The Stranglers? According to Burnel, talking to *Louder Than War* in March 2011: "The Stranglers were a prog band, a rockabilly band, a punk band, a west coast band, a psychedelic band, an arty band, or we were just The Stranglers. In the long term it's been a good thing that no-one could box us in. Most people are into music in not a tribal way, unless they got into music with a certain fashion. Surely you take elements from everywhere you come from unless you came in from the moment which we never did really."

The next few years saw The Stranglers branch out and away from the musical style that they had first became known for. With hindsight, this is hardly surprising considering the potential they displayed in 1977 — their music was more melodic and structurally more complex than many of the punk bands that they were often lumped in with.

With hindsight, in the *Louder Than War* interview Burnel said; "We were as punk as The Clash. They were just wussies and still are and we are not. Them and the Pistols were like The Monkees. They were put together by their managers and controlled by their managers and we were quite definitely not. Joe Strummer was always lovely and sweet to me. Steve and Paul from the Pistols were great also, and you might disagree the Pistols and The Clash were no better than Take That. They were fabricated music, they were exciting of course, there is no question of that but The Stranglers were organic. You would not fabricate a bloke who was fifteen years older than the rest of the band, Dave as well, Dave, and Hugh, you can't invent someone like that and also a frog immigrant with a chip on his shoulder – who is a psychopath, educated and plays classical music – you don't fabricate bands like that. You just can't."

It is worth noting perhaps, that many journalists seemed keen to capitalise on those moments when The Stranglers were having a bad day. This is noteworthy because it is just one snippet in time. That is to say, were The Stranglers a moody band who were unhappy with how things were going or did some journalists just prefer to play on the idea because it suited the angle of their own narrative aims?

For instance, it was reported in *Melody Maker* in June 1978; "JJ Burnel stalks around the table like a caged leopard as he speaks.... Hugh Cornwell stares at me from his seat at the other end of the table, his expression fixed somewhere between curiosity and hostility. They've all been angered by Harry Doherty's review of their *Black And White* album."

Burnel said; "I wanted to see Doherty here. The review was condescending and I don't like being patronised by people with smaller brains than us. We will go the same way as Jon Savage. Tell him to keep out of town." (Burnel had already punched Jon Savage after he had given them a bad review).

Martin Rushent stayed with The Stranglers to produce *Black And White* but when it came to making *The Raven*, he quit partway through. Notably, not only were The Stranglers in a different place musically by that point in their career but they were also in the depths of their problems with heroine. 1980 saw Cornwell go to prison for drug possession. It resulted in him being absent from a number of gigs at London's Rainbow. The Stranglers invited other musicians to play at the gig: Ian Dury, Hazel O'Connor, Toyah, Wilko Johnson and Phil Daniels). Just months later, all of The Stranglers were put behind bars after a riot broke out at a gig of theirs in Nice.

By the early eighties, even though The Stranglers didn't have the same commercial appeal on record compared to 1977, they still had a lot of success overall as a live band. After their 1981 album, *The Gospel According To The Meninblack*, had flopped commercially, their record label had little faith in them (United Artists had merged with EMI by that point).

It could be said that their album released later that year, *La Folie*, was their saving grace in that it featured the hit single, 'Golden Brown'. It was after this that The Stranglers left EMI in favour of Epic. Before their departure from EMI, The Stranglers offered the label one last single, 'Strange Little Girl' and *The Collection 1977-1982* album, both of which did well commercially ('Strange Little Girl' actually pre-dates The Stranglers' 1977 success, so much so that the song is joint credited to Hans Wärmling who wrote it when he was with the band in 1974).

After four more studio albums, Cornwell left The Stranglers in 1990 on the basis that his dynamic with Burnel was under strain and on account of feeling that based on The Stranglers' reputation overall, it was creatively limiting for him.

Away from The Stranglers, Cornwell has achieved solo success not only as a musician in his own right, but as an author too. To date, he has authored six books. He also has nine solo studio albums to his name.

The rest of The Stranglers chose to carry on and welcomed vocalist Paul Roberts and guitarist John Ellis to the band. Four albums later, Ellis left and was replaced by Baz Warne. After the *Norfolk Coast* album in 2004 (which spawned the hit single 'Big Thing Coming'), Roberts left the band and Warne provided vocals for The Stranglers' 2006 album, *Suite XVI*.

In 2012, they released the album, *Giants*. A highlight of The Stranglers' career in recent years has been their sell-out gig at the Roundhouse on 4th November in 2007. It marked their thirtieth anniversary and in celebration of that, the setlist stayed true to the one from a gig that they had played at the venue in 1977. Some of their more recent songs were included as part of the encore. The gig was recorded and released on the DVD, *Rattus At The Roundhouse*. The band have continued in this form to this very day with regards to touring (Jet Black is still an official member of the band but due to poor health, it is now the case that Jim Macaulay drums for them).

Understandably, in terms of the lyrics, some of The Stranglers' songs from 1977 might not have aged well for some people. Burnel told *The Quietus* in March 2014; "I remember a few years ago we did the thirtieth anniversary of the release of *Rattus Norvegicus* and we played at the Roundhouse and did the same set that we did thirty years previously and the people from *The Independent* or *The Guardian* came along and said something like, "I Feel Like A Wog' makes me feel more uncomfortable now than it did thirty years ago'."

Each to their own though, the same approach is perhaps best applied to the whole sexism thing. As Burnel said to *Louder Than War* in 2011; "I never got the sexist thing nor did any of our girlfriends. People had a strange lack of a sense of humour. The first time I encountered political correctness was when 'Peaches' had been banned by the right on Rough Trade shop because they thought it was disgusting. All these wankers take things literally. They didn't know we were smarter than any of them and not one dimensional. We hit a few nerves. We covered so many points. It reflects more on the people who were offended by The Stranglers... It was easy then and we played up to it. The fuss was pretty pathetic and eventually pretty detrimental to the band's career."

On 3rd May 2020, Dave Greenfield lost his life to coronavirus at the age of seventy-one. He contracted it whilst in hospital for a heart ailment. Horribly sad news. Thank you for the music.

The band's tour was postponed because of the virus but re-scheduled to start in October 2021 in celebration of Dave. Likewise *Dark Matters*, the band's eighteenth studio album was released 10th September 2021. Recording had begun before Greenfield's death and he appears on eight of the eleven tracks. The album is also the first not to feature Jet Black but aged eighty-three, he is still thanked in the credits.

Dark Matters charted at number four in the Official UK Chart making it the band's best performing studio album since *Feline* peaked at the same position thirty-eight years earlier.

A big shout out to all The Stranglers fans out there. As divisive as some people found The Stranglers' music in 1977, how fantastic it is to think that they did it anyway and created something that was unapologetically bold and of course, downright memorable. Over four decades later, their music lives on.

Appendices

Discography

Rattus Norvegicus

Personnel:
Hugh Cornwell - guitars, lead and backing vocals
Jean-Jacques Burnel - bass guitar, lead and backing vocals
Dave Greenfield - keyboards (Hammond L100 Organ, Hohner Cembalet electric piano, Minimoog synthesiser), backing and lead vocals
Jet Black - drums

Additional personnel:
Eric Clarke - Guest tenor saxophone (track 7)
Martin Rushent - production
Alan Winstanley - engineering
Denny King   assistance and mixing engineering
Doug Bennett - mixing engineering
Trevor Rogers - sleeve photography
Paul Henry - sleeve art direction, artwork and design

Track Listing

Side One
1. Sometimes (4:56)
2. Goodbye Toulouse (3:12)
3. London Lady (2:25)
4. Princess Of The Streets (4:34)
5. Hanging Around (4:25)

Side Two
6. Peaches (4:03)
7. (Get A) Grip (On Yourself) (3:55)
8. Ugly (4:03)
9. Down In The Sewer (7:30)

Free single:
10. Choosey Susie (3:14)
12. Peasant In The Big Shitty (3:42)*
*Live at The Nashville pub in West Kensington, 10th December 1976

Original release, 15th April 1977:
United Artists Records UAG 30045, LP
Originally with a triangular hype sticker on the sleeve shrink wrap (not always applied accurately to top left corner) indicating "Includes Free Single - Limited Edition" (first 10,000, 7" housed in a plain dark-orange/red sleeve).
United Artists Records TCK 30045, cassette

Reissues:
EMI, FA 3001, LP, 1982
EMI, TC-FA 3001, cassette, 1982
EMI, CDP 7 46362 2, CD, 1988
EMI, PRDFCD 5, CD, 1996
With bonus tracks: Choosey Susie (3:14) / Go Buddy Go (3:58) / Peasant In The Big Shitty (Live 10th Dec 1976) (3:42) //
Two versions were released, one with the bonus tracks on a separate disc.

EMI SVLP 291, LP, 2000
EMI 7243 5 34406 2 6, CD, 6th November 2001
* With bonus tracks: Choosey Susie (3:14) / Go Buddy Go (3:58) / Peasant In The Big Shitty (Live 10th Dec 1976) (3:42) //

Self- release CGLP1, LP, 27th April 2015
Initial pressing strictly limited to 500 individually numbered copies on heavyweight 180g vinyl housed in original inner sleeves. In addition, each limited album also includes a reproduction of the SIS lyric sheet and a reprint of the original album promo poster (nearly 2' in height).

Parlophone 0190295892586, CD, 2nd March 2018
With bonus tracks: Choosey Susie (3:13) / Peasant In The Big Shitty (Live) (3:39) / Go Buddy Go (3:58) / Peaches (Airplay Version) (4:07) / Grip '89 (Get A) Grip (On Yourself) (4:01) / Grip '89 (Grippin' Stuff 12" Mix) (5:38) //

No More Heroes

Personnel:
Hugh Cornwell - guitars, lead and backing vocals
Jean-Jacques Burnel - bass guitar, lead and backing vocals
Dave Greenfield - keyboards (Hammond L100 Organ, Hohner Cembalet electric piano, Minimoog synthesiser), lead and backing vocals
Jet Black - drums

Technical personnel:
Martin Rushent - production
Alan Winstanley - engineering
Nigel Brooke-Harte - mixing, engineering assistance
Doug Bennett - mixing
JONZ (John Dent) - mastering
Eamonn O'Keefe - sleeve photography solarisation
Trevor Rogers - sleeve photography
The Red Room - artwork design
Paul Henry - sleeve design and art direction

Track Listing

Side One
1. I Feel Like A Wog (3:16)
2. Bitching (4:25)
3. Dead Ringer (2:46)
4. Dagenham Dave (3:18)
5. Bring On The Nubiles (2:15)
6. Something Better Change (3:35)

Side Two
7. No More Heroes (3:27)
8. Peasant In The Big Shitty (3:25)
9. Burning Up Time (2:25)
10. English Towns (2:13)
11. School Mam (6:52)

Original release 23rd September 1977:
United Artists Records UAG 30200, LP
United Artists Records TCK 30200, cassette

Reissues:
EMI CDP 7 46613 2, CD, 1987
EMI FA 3190, LP, 1988
EMI TC-FA 3190, cassette, 1988
EMI 7243 8 52265 2 6, CD, 1996
With bonus tracks: Straighten Out (2:46) / 5 Minutes (3:18) / Rok It To The Moon (2:47) //

EMI 7243 5 34407 2 5, CD, 2001
With bonus tracks: Straighten Out (2:46) / 5 Minutes (3:18) / Rok It To The Moon (2:47) //

Self-release CGLP2, LP, 2015
Parlophone 0190295892548, CD, 2nd March 2018
With bonus tracks: Straighten Out (2:46) / In The Shadows (4:37) / 5 Minutes (3:17) / Rok It To The Moon (2:47) / No More Heroes (Edit) (2:56)

Live At The Hope And Anchor
EMI CDP 7987892, CD, 9th March 1992
Recorded on November 22nd, 1977 at the Hope & Anchor in Islington, North London. Tracks: Tits (5:38) / Choosey Susie (3:01) / Goodbye Toulouse (3:23) / Bitching (4:15) / Mean To Me (2:29) / School Mam (5:53) / Peasant In The Big Shitty (3:33) / In The Shadows (4:31) / Walk On By (5:36) / Princess Of The Streets (4:52) / Go Buddy Go (7:07) / No More Heroes (3:37) / Straighten Out (2:55) / Peaches (3:42) / Hanging Around (4:11) / Dagenham Dave (3:15) / Sometimes (4:56) / Bring On The Nubiles (2:27) / London Lady (2:22) //

SINGLES

Grip / London Lady
United Artists Records UP 36211, 28th January 1977

Peaches / Go Buddy Go
United Artists Records UP 36248, 6th May 1977

Something Better Change / Straighten Out
United Artists Records UP 36277, 22nd July 1977

No More Heroes / In The Shadows
United Artists Records UP 36300, 16th September 1977

Tour Dates

Throughout 1977, numerous scheduled gigs were cancelled — mainly due to The Stranglers not being welcome at some venues — as a result, whilst I have endeavoured to corroborate the following dates with ticket stubs and gig reviews where possible, please be aware that, to some extent, the following list is plausibly not exhaustive.

Sunday 2nd January	The Roundhouse, London, England
Sunday 16th January	Skindles Hotel, Maidenhead, England
Thursday 20th January	Red Deer, Croydon, England
Friday 21st January	Royal College of Art, London, England
Saturday 22nd January	The Roxy Club, London, England
Monday 24th January	Toby Jug, Tolworth, England
Saturday 29th January	Salliscenny Hall, Brighton, England
Sunday 30th January	Rainbow Theatre, London, England
Tuesday 1st February	Markethalle, Hamburg, Germany
Wednesday 2nd February	Markethalle, Hamburg, Germany *(unconfirmed)*
Wednesday 9th February	Central Halls, Woking, England
Thursday 10th February	Clouds, Edinburgh, Scotland
Friday 11th February	Robert Gordon Institute, Aberdeen, Scotland
Saturday 12th February	Queen Margaret University, Glasgow, Scotland
Monday 14th February	Hope & Anchor, London, England
Tuesday 15th February	Alexandra Club, Newport, Wales
Friday 18th February	Technical College, Crawley, England
Saturday 19th February	Priory Hotel, Scunthorpe, England
Monday 21st February	Keynes College University, Canterbury, England
Tuesday 22nd February	University of Essex, Colchester, England
Wednesday 23rd February	Polytechnic, Newcastle, England
Thursday 24th February	Rock Garden, Middlesbrough, England
Friday 25th February	Penthouse, Scarborough, England
Saturday 26th February	Eric's, Liverpool, England
Monday 28th February	Outlooks, Doncaster, England
Tuesday 1st March	Barbarella's, Birmingham, England
Thursday 3rd March	Polytechnic, Huddersfield, England
Friday 4th March	Lafayette, Wolverhampton, England
Saturday 5th March	Electric Circus, Manchester, England
Sunday 6th March	Tow Bar Inn, Cumbria, England
Monday 7th March	Tower Hotel, Hawick Scotland
Tuesday 8th March	Barbarella's, Birmingham, England
Wednesday 9th March	Unity Hall, Wakefield, England
Thursday 10th March	University, York, England
Friday 11th March	Penny Farthing, Ulverston, England
Saturday 12th March	C.F. Mott College, Liverpool, England

Wednesday 16th March	The Affair, Swindon, England
Thursday 17th March	Manor Ballroom, Ipswich, England *(cancelled)*
Friday 18th March	Sussex Centre, Brighton, England
Monday 21st March	Top Of The World, Stafford, England
Tuesday 22nd March	Drones Club, Bridgend, Wales
Wednesday 23rd March	Woods Centre, Plymouth, England
Thursday 24th March	Winter Gardens, Penzance, England
Monday 28th March	The Roxy Club, London, England
Tuesday 29th March	The Roxy Club, London, England
Wednesday 30th March	Incognito, Darlington, England
Friday 1st April	Polytechnic, Leeds, England
Saturday 2nd April	Tow Bar Inn, Cumbria, England
Wednesday 6th April	The Roundabout, Newport, Wales
Monday 11th April	The Buccaneer, Brighton, England
Thursday 14th April	Bristol, England *(cancelled)*
Friday 15th April	Sports Centre, Bracknell, England *(cancelled)*
Saturday 16th April	The Roundhouse, London, England
Sunday 17th April	The Roundhouse, London, England
Monday 2nd May	The Nashville, London, England
Wednesday 11th May	Winning Post, Twickenham, England
Friday 13th May	Eric's, Liverpool, England
Saturday 14th May	Herriot Watt, Edinburgh, Scotland
Sunday 15th May	Maxim's, Barrow, England
Thursday 19th May	Tiffany's, Coventry, England
Friday 20th May	Brunel University, Uxbridge, England
Saturday 21st May	Sports Centre, Bletchley, England
Sunday 22nd May	Greyhound, Croydon, England *(cancelled)*
Tuesday 24th May	Top Rank, Brighton, England
Wednesday 25th May	University of Essex, Colchester, England
Thursday 26th May	St Andrew's Hall, Norwich, England
Friday 27th May	Top Rank, Cardiff, Wales
Saturday 28th May	Odeon, Canterbury, England
Sunday 29th May	Civic Hall, Guildford, England
Monday 30th May	Village Bowl, Bournemouth, England
Tuesday 31st May	Civic Hall, Wolverhampton, England
Wednesday 1st June	Barbarella's, Birmingham, England
Thursday 2nd June	Barbarella's, Birmingham, England
Friday 3rd June	Corn Exchange, Cambridge, England
Saturday 4th June	Casino, Wigan, England
Sunday 5th June	Electric Circus, Manchester, England
Tuesday 7th June	Odeon, Taunton, England
Wednesday 8th June	Castaways, Plymouth, England
Thursday 9th June	Town Hall, Torquay, England *(cancelled)*
Friday 10th June	Grand Pavilion, Llandrindod Wells, Wales
Saturday 11th June	California Ballroom, Dunstable, England
Sunday 12th June	Top Rank, Sheffield, England

Monday 13th June	St George's Hall, Bradford, England
Tuesday 14th June	Tiffany's, Shrewsbury, England
Wednesday 15th June	City Hall, Newcastle, England
Thursday 16th June	Town Hall, Middlesbrough, England
Friday 17th June	Gaumont, Doncaster, England
Saturday 18th June	Imperial Hotel, Blackpool, England *(cancelled)*
Sunday 19th June	Eric's, Liverpool, England *(two shows)*
Monday 20th June	Top Of The World, Stafford, England
Tuesday 21st June	Victoria Halls, Stoke On Trent, England
Wednesday 22nd June	City Hall, Glasgow, Scotland

Thursday 23rd June	Winter Gardens, Cleethorpes, England
Friday 24th June	Bristol Exhibition Centre, England *(cancelled)*
Saturday 25th June	Civic Hall, St Albans, England *(cancelled)*
Sunday 26th June	The Roundhouse, London, England *(two shows)*
Saturday 27th August	Wilmot Youth Centre, Finchley, London, England
Friday 2nd September	Paradiso Club, Amsterdam, Netherlands
?? September	Kilppan, Sweden
Wednesday 7th September	Eksit Club, Rotterdam, Netherlands
Thursday 8th September	Paradiso Club, Amsterdam, Netherlands
Friday 9th September	Volksbildungsheim, Frankfurt, Germany
Sunday 11th September	Winterhauder, Hamburg, Germany
Wednesday 14th September	Stockholm University, Sweden
Friday 23rd September	Corn Exchange, Cambridge, England
Saturday 24th September	Bracknell Sports Centre, England
Sunday 25th September	Odeon, Canterbury, England
Monday 26th September	Polytechnic, Oxford, England
Tuesday 27th September	St Andrew's Hall, Norwich, England
Wednesday 28th September	Gaumont, Ipswich, England
Thursday 29th September	Brunel Sports Centre, Uxbridge, England
Friday 30th September	Sports Centre, Crawley, England

Saturday 1st October	Kursaal, Southend, England
Sunday 2nd October	Queensway Hall, Dunstable, England
Monday 3rd October	De Montfort Hall, Leicester, England
Tuesday 4th October	Locarno, Coventry, England
Wednesday 5th October	St Peter's Hall, Carmarthen, Wales
Thursday 6th October	Winter Gardens, Malvern, England
Saturday 8th October	University, Bangor, Wales
Sunday 9th October	Fiesta, Plymouth, England
Monday 10th October	University, Exeter, England
Wednesday 12th October	City Hall, Newcastle, England

Thursday 13th October	Apollo, Manchester, England
Friday 14th October	University, Liverpool, England
Saturday 15th October	Queens Hall, Leeds, England
Sunday 16th October	Apollo, Glasgow, Scotland
Monday 17th October	The Market, Carlisle, England
Wednesday 19th October	Top Rank, Sheffield, England
Thursday 20th October	Mayfair Suite, Birmingham, England
Friday 21st October	Victoria Hall, Hanley, England
Saturday 22nd October	Exhibition Centre, Bristol, England
Sunday 23rd October	Top Rank, Cardiff, Wales
Monday 24th October	Top Rank, Swansea, Wales
Wednesday 26th October	Top Rank, Brighton, England
Thursday 27th October	Village Bowl, Bournemouth, England
Friday 28th October	Surrey University, Guildford, England
Saturday 29th October	Pier Pavilion, Hastings, England
Sunday 30th October	Top Rank, Reading, England
Monday 31st October	Top Rank, Southampton, England

Wednesday 2nd November	The Roundhouse, London, England
Thursday 3rd November	The Roundhouse, London, England
Friday 4th November	The Roundhouse, London, England
Saturday 5th November	The Roundhouse, London, England

Sunday 6th November	The Roundhouse, London, England
Wednesday 9th November	Ulster Hall, Belfast, Northern Ireland *(cancelled)*
Thursday 10th November	University of Ulster, Coleraine, Northern Ireland
Friday 11th November	Trinity College, Dublin, Ireland
Saturday 12th November	The Stadium, Dublin, Ireland *(cancelled)*
Sunday 13th November	City Hall, Cork, Ireland
Monday 14th November	Dublin Trinity College, Ireland
Tuesday 22nd November	Hope & Anchor, London, England
Sunday 27th November	Paradiso Club, Amsterdam, Netherlands
Monday 28th November	Paradiso Club, Amsterdam, Netherlands

About The Author

Laura Shenton MA LLCM DipRSL has been thinking about music since she first heard it, possibly whilst still in the womb. She has a Masters degree in "Music Since 1900" from Liverpool Hope University. Her hobbies and interests include writing, playing the piano, staying up into the small hours wondering about life whilst eating crisps and obsessing about music, hamsters and dogs. In particular, her writing buddy is the best dog in the world — a black Labrador.